Advance Praise for *The Roadmap to Freedom*

"As entrepreneurs soon find out, there's a big difference between starting a company and leading one. If you're getting bogged down in day-to-day firefighting, let Chris McIntyre's excellent guide show you how to put systems in place that will free you to focus on your passions again."

—Ken Blanchard, co-author of *The One Minute Manager®* and *Leading at a Higher Level*

"If you're a small-business owner looking to get the best (not the most . . .) out of your team—you'd be NUTS not to read this book!"

—Dr.'s Kevin and Jackie Freiberg *The New York Times* bestselling authors of *NUTS* and *Nanovation*

"This book is the cure for that crazy-busy, small-business owner who realizes they need a better system to get to that next level."

—Steve Strauss, senior columnist *USA Today*

"The Roadmap to Freedom *is the most complete small- to mid-sized business owner leadership book out there. This one is a must for any owner who is serious about world-class leadership. We're bringing Chris back again."*

—Rick Wolfe, Event Chair, YPO Florida Chapter

Tiffany!
Thank you for your friendship & constant support throughout the years. Here's to your continued success in 2013!!
Chris McIntyre
12/15/12

"I knew Chris was an exceptional speaker and coach, so I'm surprised that I was . . . surprised . . . about how effective The Roadmap to Freedom *is. This book shows you how to get 'that thing' out of your head—and into the minds of your people . . . ."*

—Dan Doyle, CEO, DEX Imaging

"I've been in business for 32 years now, and I haven't seen a roadmap this clear, concise, and just plain old helpful! Great read! Thanks for getting this out there for business owners like me!"

—Randy Sinclair, CEO, RanRoy Printing Company

"If it wasn't for our systematic approach to synergizing a bunch of dedicated individuals into a cohesive team, we wouldn't have won Gold in 2010. McIntyre's 'mantra' method shows you how to align your team with a message that will bring home the Gold in your business."

—Steve Mesler, 2010 Bobsled Gold Medalist and Corporate Consultant

THE ROADMAP TO FREEDOM

a small-business owner's guide to connecting people to a **core message**

CHRIS MCINTYRE

Ep
Entrepreneur
PRESS®

Publisher: Entrepreneur Press
Cover Design: Andrew Welyczko
Composition and production: Eliot House Productions

Library of Congress Cataloging-in-Publication Data
McIntyre, Chris, 1974–
The roadmap to freedom: a small-business owner's guide to connecting people to a core message / by Chris McIntyre.
p. cm.
ISBN-13: 978-1-59918-493-7
ISBN-10: 1-59918-493-1 (alk. paper)
1. Small business—Management. 2. Small business—Personnel management. 3. Employees—Recruiting. I. Title.
HD62.7.M3946 2012
658.02'2—dc23 2012015998

Printed in the United States of America

17 16 15 14 13 10 9 8 7 6 5 4 3 2 1

Dedication

I'd first like to thank my mom, Mary McIntyre, for all of her consistently selfless contributions throughout the years. As a single mother, I can't even begin to comprehend the sacrifices you've made. Just know that because of you, this book IS! Thank you. I love you.

A second special thank you goes out to all of the small-business owners who graciously donated their time and expertise during the interviews for this book. This book would not have been possible if it weren't for you.

Third, I'd like to thank my good friend and mentor Ed Gallagher. Your "three-questions," humility, and constant support have been invaluable. I'd follow you into battle any day.

Finally, this book is for all small- to mid-sized business owners out there. You had the guts to go for it in life. One of the things I admire most is effort—and you own it. I salute you.

Contents

Part II

Create Your Core Mantra

Part IV
Appendices

Preface

The "Freedom" Trap

Small-Business Owners (SBOs) typically go into business with excitement, determination, and a seductive vision of the "total freedom" business success can give them. With lots of hard work, a strong vision, and maybe even a dash of luck, the business takes flight and does even better than expected. That success, though, tends to illuminate the blurry, informal, and often incomplete internal systems and processes. The performance agreements made by the boss, spouse, old college buddies, and whoever else might have been there from the start are simply no longer sufficient. What then?

SBOs are often uniquely prepared to create and deliver their product or service. Unfortunately, most SBOs are usually far less equipped to effectively lead, let alone develop, their team. Often they struggle to align people with brand, handle performance management issues, and effectively manage the boss/buddy relationships required in such a tight environment. They can never find the time to create effective people systems let alone make sense of the abyss of ever-changing roles and responsibilities. And let's not even think about what's happening to their personal life and relationships.

It's official: The SBOs become a victim of their own *"success,"* trapped by the demands of the business in their pursuit of—freedom.

Enter *The Roadmap to Freedom*, an engaging series of four, do-it-yourself styled books that facilitate a SBOs transition from chief doer and knowledge holder to Chief Executive Overseer.

Here is the *Roadmap to Freedom*: Connect + Motivate + Systemize + Focus

- **Step 1: *Connect People to the Core***
- **Step 2: *Lead and Motivate without Money***
- **Step 3: *Systemize Your Success***
- **Step 4: *Focus on Freedom***

Strategically, *The Roadmap to Freedom* series walks SBOs through how to (1) connect the right team to a consistent message, (2) create, lead, and motivate high performers, (3) automate business processes, and (4) how to get UN-Busy, and actually enjoy your newfound freedom.

Tactically, these books will offer SBOs a clear way to consistently put legs beneath their strategies. Specifically, you'll find a step-by-step blueprint for:

- Building a core team of superstars
- Guaranteeing others care as much about the goals as you do
- Involving your team in the development of an accountability process they'll own
- Clarifying and harmonizing ever-changing roles and responsibilities
- Motivating friends and family members without the use of money
- Forming ego-free communication agreements from the top down
- Providing stability during the storms of economic uncertainty
- Enjoying freedom in a world of infinite opportunity

Most leadership books focus on life in the corporate world, with multimillion dollar training budgets, HR offices, and layers of staff. This series, on the other hand, was written specifically with the uniqueness of the small-business context and resources in mind. It will help provide SBOs with the infrastructure necessary for the next phases of their business's growth.

The tools, insights, and strategies you'll learn in this series were developed through in-depth interviews with successful SBOs across the U.S., as well as my firsthand experiences coaching senior leaders around the world. My hope is that this series will serve as the "missing manual" for America's small- to mid-sized business owners and organizational leaders. I also trust it will be an equally useful resource to help your superstars understand the role they play in contributing to a world-class team.

This book and the entire *Roadmap to Freedom* series, is meant to offer you a template to be modified based on your leadership philosophy, your team's input, and your distinct business model. To that end, you will find pop quizzes to help focus your attention on key areas. Summary checklists at the end of every chapter will guide you in facilitating a meaningful dialogue with your team and developing your own tailored action plan.

You can download every checklist, tool, and form in this book for free from my website at www.christophermcintyre.com. There, you can also download the full audio interviews I did with SBOs from across the country. I look forward to hearing your ideas and comments on my blogs. Until then—enjoy, and let's get started.

Part I

Craft Your Core Team

In order for your business to successfully grow from a handful of people to a fully functioning team of 15-200+ personnel, you need to make sure you find and hire the *right* core people. How do you attract superstars? How do you keep them? How do you get rid of the people who may become a nightmare for your business?

Part I of this book answers those questions by helping you identify the right kind of talent for your business and how to keep them. Through a systematic approach, you can identify and engage the right personnel and know when to drop those that won't measure up to your standards.

Creating a trusted on-boarding—and-off boarding—process is key to your long-term freedom. People are the key foundation of your business, so you need to know how to get it right. If you already have a rock-solid process for attracting and keeping superstars and dropping nightmares, you might just want to answer the Chapter 1, 2 and 3 summary checklists—and jump right into *Part II: Create Your Core Mantra.*

If you don't have a trusted process for getting and keeping only the best people—read on.

Chapter 1

How to Attract Superstars

Attract superstars. Keep superstars. Drop nightmares like a hot rock. Owning the right raw elements really is that basic. Simple? Yes. Easy? No way. If it were easy everyone would be doing it, and let's face it, very few small-business owners (SBOs) have what they would consider to be a "Dream Team."

For clarity—let's borrow a couple definitions from dictionary.com:

> *Superstar:* a person, or thing, esteemed for exceptional talent, and eagerly sought for services.
>
> *Nightmare:* an event, or experience, that is intensely distressing.

Superstars are good. They are capable, interested, and genuine contributors to your vision. I realize everyone has bad days, including the boss. But from this point forward let's loosely refer to superstars as all the people on your team who are not consistently a nightmare. Superstars—or those with superstar potential to work

> **POP QUIZ**
>
> Is your team a *super-star team* or an overly vocal gaggle of jaded, disengaged, burnt-out nightmares? Or maybe you have a mediocre mix of all of the above, depending on the day?

with and develop—should be the only ones left after you implement the processes you will find in this book.

Nightmares are . . . *nightmares*. They consistently bring cloudy, energy-draining, distressing experiences your way. Notice, though, that in defining a nightmare we're focusing on *events* or *experiences*. It's not that nightmares are bad people. Our definition looks more at the consequence of actions and behaviors—not people. That's an important distinction to make right upfront.

Talent issues continue to nag SBOs because we can be programmed to favor the wrong skills. As you can see in Figure 1.1, the Department of Labor estimates that up to 80 percent of job success is based not on knowledge and technical skills, but on people skills, work ethics, and attitudes, or PEAs.

Figure 1.1—**Department of Labor Job Success Estimates**

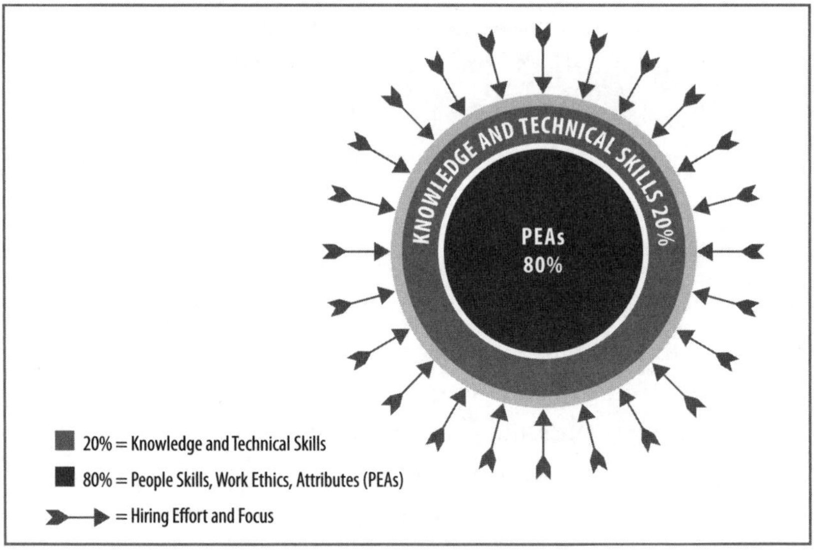

Stop Hitting the Wrong Targets

If you're like most SBOs, you've probably spent 80 percent of your focus challenging potential new hires to prove they've mastered the wrong (knowledge and technical) skills. In other words, you may be hitting the target but ignoring the bull's-eye.

One reason SBOs consistently miss the bull's-eye is because they place more emphasis on *what* was achieved rather than on *how* it was achieved. Why? The results are usually easier to see. It's easy to point to completed projects, decreased errors, and increased sales. Those things are objective. You can see, touch, count, review, inspect, and measure them. But how do you measure passion? How do you count trust? How do you inspect empathy?

Those PEAs, commonly referred to as "soft skills," are more ambiguous and take more thought to objectify. You might not even be sure about how best to clarify or measure the most important stuff. It may be that a large percentage of your new hire's potential for success isn't being communicated or measured. Ironically, the PEAs may be the primary things you expect from your employees.

Defining all of the knowledge, skills, and PEAs necessary for success in your business is tough—but it can be done. By doing so, you give yourself maximum opportunity to find the right kind of superstar. Are you able to objectify (write down and list) *all* of the metrics and PEAs most necessary for success in the unique culture of your business?

> **MEET THE HEROES**
> You can read an overview of the SBOs interviewed for this book in Appendix A.

Sometimes what you ask for isn't what you need. The basic requirements that most SBOs ask for—such as degrees, computer wizardry, and business fundamentals—say nothing about *how* new team members are expected to make their impact. James Carter, CEO of Be Legendary, a team-building company (www.belegenendary.org), learned this lesson the hard way when he realized:

The passion to create a better world wasn't in my first partner's makeup. It wasn't one of his guiding principles.

James' partner was a bona fide genius with an exceptional achievement-based resume. Unfortunately, he wasn't connected to the kind of impact James wanted to have on the community and the world. That lack of genuine connection to a bigger purpose created a constant tension between managing the books and managing toward the vision. James got exactly what he asked for, but he hadn't asked for what the business needed most.

THESE QUESTIONS CAN UNCOVER PEAS

- Can you remember a time when your work ethic really contributed to a business goal?
- Share an example of a time when your attitude inspired a team to go in a different direction—and achieved a positive outcome. Where were they headed? Where did they go?
- Can you share an example of how you recently handled a mistake?
- Share one instance of a time when you actually compromised your own personal values. What was the value? How did you later address the issue?

Define the Key PEAs

Attracting true superstars is easier if you're able to define 100 percent of the key skills and attributes you expect to see in action. Is it passion? Trust? Integrity? Work ethic? It may even be empathy or exceptional communication. Whatever it is, define it.

Here is one possible definition of *passion*:

A consistent and genuinely excited intent to make a positive difference.

A few key words will need clarification. *Consistent, genuine, excited, intent,* and even *positive* are all words that could be misperceived. Is *consistent* once a week or once a year? Does *genuine* mean just doing it well enough to squeak by?

Words like *intent* put less focus on *what* was achieved and more on *how* it was attempted. *What* was done and *how* it was done are both critical elements worthy of focused feedback. Later in the book, I'll introduce a performance management system that clearly identifies and connects *what* was achieved with *how* it was achieved.

Obviously, the end result is absolutely critical. But I want to highlight the fact that world-class teams only partially focus on results. When you follow the right systematic process, the results will come. Focusing on processes as well as results will allow you to reward hard work, effort, and intent (and PEAs)—even during times of miserable failure.

There's no magic bullet here. But simply trying to define key soft skills can raise your team's collective consciousness about what's most important. Having that conversation also enables the team to better align with and contribute to your vision.

One easy way to clarify the concept of PEAs is to ask what they look like in action—and not in action. Figure 1.2 on page 8 can help you define and measure key PEAs you want to see more of in your business.

You may consider choosing a few examples of PEAs you feel are most important—and then asking your team to do the same. Then, meet with your team and go through a process of elimination until you agree on a few competencies that are most important for success in your business.

We will get to defining and measuring key PEAs much more deeply in Part II. For now, just be curious about how much of what's really necessary for success (such as being ready to engage, serve, care, and empathize) is currently not being requested. Now that you have your list of key PEAs, the next step is to align them.

Figure 1.2—Measuring People Skills, Work Ethics, and Attributes (PEAs)

WHAT'S MOST IMPORTANT HERE		
Key PEAs	**In Action**	**Not in Action**
Passion	Giving the customer a ride home	Pretending you didn't hear the customer say they had no ride
Empathy	Bringing co-worker flowers because her cat died	Joking that you thought cats had nine lives
Work Ethic	Staying late to show Ben how to create formulas in Excel	Leaving early because it's "Ben's job" to figure it out
Others		
Others		

Align the PEAs with Performance Metrics

Well-defined soft skills should be consistently aligned with the most important strategic goals and assets. Passion is great, but someone could be *passionate* about being a gang member, terrorist, or identity thief. Just identifying the skills you want isn't enough, you've got to define and strategically connect your team to them.

Let's go back to James for a minute. James' first business partner was more *passionate* about "the bottom line" than about making a difference in the lives of the company's customers. Increasing the bottom line did bring in more revenue in the short run, but a lack of attention to customer needs leads to less-satisfied customers and lost revenue in the long run.

> **FREE PEAs**
> You can find a great list of potential PEAs in Appendix B.

Defining and aligning soft skills with clear goals and checking in consistently is a *process* that will lead to positive *results*. Defining the soft stuff also provides more perspective about everything that's important, not just the easily measured stuff. The third part of this book will show you exactly how to align those PEAs directly with your most valuable assets.

The point here is to be curious about how well you're currently able to articulate, measure, and connect all the skills most necessary for success in your business. This is critical because when you start trying to find talent you will be able to more concisely ask superstars to prove they know how to hit the bull's-eye.

Doing an Online and Social Media Search

When writing this section, I was a bit hesitant to mention specific social media sites for fear of dating this book. My concern was that if I mentioned specific sites now, they may be obsolete in a year. But I'm going to do it anyway because leveraging social media is absolutely critical to finding top talent. Here are a few common questions SBOs tend to have regarding social media.

Social Media Question #1: What Social Media Should I Consider?

In no particular order, here are a few ways you can leverage some popular sites to find superstars:

- *Twitter and Facebook.* Post positions and ask "followers/friends" if they know someone who knows someone.
- *LinkedIn.* More than 150 million superstar candidates easily accessible. More on LinkedIn later.
- *Jobvite.* Focuses recruiting efforts on developing referrals from your own employees and their social media networks. (There is a fee.)
- *YouTube.* Can get video answers and click-by-click instructions on how to do anything (including how to use any of the sites I've mentioned above).

Social Media Question #2: How Can I Use LinkedIn to Find Superstars?

LinkedIn, if you're not already aware of it, is kind of like a Facebook page—but for professionals. You may not have the time, or interest, to learn about all the site has to offer—but here are a few particularly useful LinkedIn functions.

- Search for key words (sales, training, etc.) and view work history, recent tweets (Twitter), and testimonials of potential superstars.
- Export contact info of your direct connections and send personalized emails.
- Find "warm" leads by viewing the direct connections of those you're LinkedIn with, called first-level connections.
- See shared connections that you might not have been aware of.
- Do an advanced search (with a premium account) of your connections three levels deep—view names, bios, and contact people directly.
- Post targeted searches using corporate recruiting solutions (talent.linkedin.com).
- Watch free webcasts on how to make an effective LinkedIn search.
- Use an app on your smartphone, such as cardmunch, to take a picture of a business card and have it automatically converted to a LinkedIn contact.

Social Media Question #3: How Do I Stay Current with All the Latest Social Media Tools?

The quick answer: Good luck with that! Accept the fact that online tools—and social media in particular—are in a constant state of change. You're too busy to constantly be chasing all the latest tips and tricks. However, you will need to maintain a functional understanding of some of the potential superstar search options available to you. Here are a few "timeless" things you can do, or ask, now or 15 years from now to help you quickly get up to speed:

- Dig up the professional association that governs your industry. Call and ask them how they leverage social media and online job boards (i.e., www.indeed.com, www.monster.com, etc.).
- Call staffing agencies and recruiters for the position you're trying to fill and ask them the same questions.
- Ask your local chamber of commerce and employee development departments about upcoming job fairs. Go there and network with hiring managers.
- Subscribe to magazines oriented toward small businesses (*Entrepreneur*, *Inc.*)—and go to their annual and/or marketing events (where you can talk to fellow entrepreneurs).

Don't be afraid to hire a social media professional, or find one for cheap at a local college campus. I hired an expert, Nancy Shed (find her on LinkedIn), and she's a giant reason you're reading this book right now.

Finding Superstars Offline

Yes, social media can connect you with potential superstars you wouldn't typically have had a chance to meet. But don't forget about the good old-fashioned, face-to-face approach either. In addition to using social media here are a few more ways you can find superstar talent.

Make Superstars Look for You

Imagine what life would be like if superstar employees were always begging to work for you. If they're not doing that, I challenge you to figure out *why* they're not. Getting noticed by the best happens more when you're the best. Being the best puts you on the mountaintop, and that means superstars will seek you out.

Here are some questions that might help:

- Do superstars seek us out? Why? Why not?

- What is it about working here that differentiates us from our competition?
- What indicators do we consistently reference to keep tabs on our reputation?
- How might those indicators be changing (i.e., social media)?
- What are a couple of reasons a superstar would not choose us (other than salary)? What can we do about it?

Being the best means you're less likely to have to do battle with the mass of mediocre competitors out there. The value of clarifying why you're not currently "the best" in the minds of superstars could highlight a competitive advantage your competition currently has on you. You may want to try to plug that hole first.

Two Degrees of Separation

In 1929 Hungarian poet Frigyes Karinthy suggested you could access anyone on the planet through leveraging no more than six different people; this became popularly known as "six degrees of separation." I'd bet the right kind of talent for your business is less than two degrees of separation from you right now, especially if you count digital social networking alternatives. In other words, someone you know personally knows someone you might want to hire.

In leveraging two degrees of separation, I found 16 successful SBOs from across the country willing to help with the interviews for this book in just three days. By that, I mean that 16 out of the 17 CEOs I interviewed for this book were either my personal friends or personal friends of one of my personal friends. How many contacts do you currently have in your contacts list? If you're one of those SBOs with hundreds—or even thousands—of contacts, I guarantee all your staffing needs are sitting right there under your nose.

Don't be afraid to network in-house, too. Leverage your current superstars for who they know. Most superstars know other superstars. Chances are they can connect you to a new addition they would be willing to work with. Even if you're not ready to hire, it may be useful to always have lists of possible hires standing by, like the major airlines do.

Overbook Just Like the Airlines

Phil Coady, CEO of Microgroove (www.microgroove.com) software development company, said he likens the superstar hiring process to "overbooking like the airlines do." I love his concept.

Why not find talent before you need to? Attend trade shows and loiter (physically and digitally) around the halls of professional organizations and forums within your industry. You might also check in with vendors, suppliers, and other trusted contacts associated with your craft.

By periodically cycling through sections of your contacts, you'll be able to stay connected to the talent pool, and you'll find yourself less frequently in a hiring rut without options. I've seen SBOs who functionally categorized their contact lists by "Vendors," "Sales Folks," "Suppliers," or "Engineers." Would you benefit by grouping potential networking lists based on function or position? Possible categories for your contacts are shown in Figure 1.3 on page 14.

All that said, Phil also mentioned that he has far more competent people available than he ever expects to need to fill a position in a hurry. He doesn't like to hurry when hiring. He's had the most success partnering with people as outside consultants before formally bringing them onto the team.

You may want to check in with one or two contacts, per category, every month or so. Maybe one month you could check in with a few vendors,

POP QUIZ

Do you have a list of three potential superstars to backfill every position in your business? If not, are you at least staying fairly well connected to your contacts? You may find value in cycling through functional categories periodically.

Figure 1.3—**Functionally Group or Label Your Contact List**

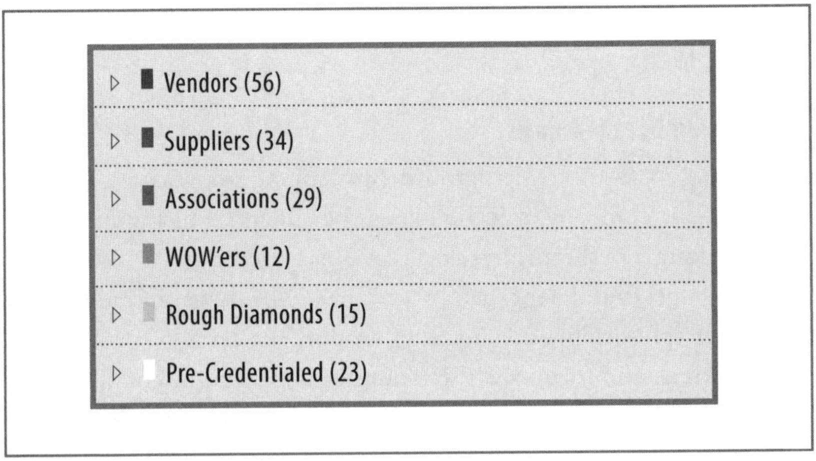

just to say hello. The following month, you might communicate with a few key suppliers. The goal is to keep potential leads warm in case you ever need to find a new superstar.

Always Hiring: WOW'ers

Steven Jones–CEO of Jones and Associates Consulting, a Diversity Consulting Firm (www.jandaconsult.com)–suggested:

> *One of our criteria for hiring people is when they walk into a room the response of people is "WOW . . . I want to listen to that person." Those folks have flexibility, humility, and their egos in check. They're already living their purpose and part of that purpose is bridging the divide. They've got the talent. Their personal work is done and they have the intellectual rigor and communication skills to take complicated issues and present them in a simple way that moves people to action.*

Have you ever had an encounter with someone who made you say, "WOW–she was great!" Maybe you received exceptional service in a restaurant or at a hotel. Or perhaps you just heard an outstanding speech. You might even have seen someone hand a stranger back his dropped wallet or give up his seat on the subway to someone elderly. Notice these people and get connected with them. Look for the WOW'ers wherever you are. Add them to your contacts list.

When was the last time you passed up the opportunity to add a WOW'er to your contacts list? Have you ever *not* been WOW'd by someone *with* a formal credential next to her name? Just because someone has a degree doesn't mean they're a superstar. On the other side of that argument, WOW'ers don't always have one of those fancy degrees.

Dig Up Rough Diamonds and Pre-Credentialed Superstars

You should regard a down economy as an ideal time to find cheap diamonds. Part of the value of economic turmoil and high unemployment is that superstar talent can be purchased for minimal cost. People get laid off from jobs they've had for decades. Many of those folks never needed degrees and now find themselves stuck because they don't have "formal" credentials. Those highly skilled folks are diamonds in the rough. Use your two degrees to focus on finding them.

Similarly, don't be afraid to take a risk on the pre-credentialed crowd. From my perspective, pre-credentialed means someone without the latest degree or fancy certification. Maybe they currently lack certain technical skills but have WOW people skills. Hire for the WOW and be flexible enough to teach the *how*. By being willing to take risks on potential talent, you can create their loyalty.

The pre-credentialed talent pool offers the biggest bang for your buck. These are the superstars who will shine soon regardless of where they land, so you may as well get them before your competition does. Plant, water, and grow them from within.

Warning! The pre-credented pool offers amazing value—but also greater potential risk. Always remember that there's no getting around the need for a rock-solid hiring process to ensure you filter out the wild cards.

Six-Step Air-Tight Superstar Hiring Process

How solid is your current hiring process? On a scale of 1 to 10, how would you rate it? Obviously, one of the best ways to get the right talent on board is to have a trusted hiring process in place. Here is a six-step process that you can adopt as is, or tailor to meet your needs.

Step #1: Define the Knowledge, Skills, and PEAs

You probably have a good sense of the hard objectives you expect your applicants to achieve (i.e., *x* percent increase in sales; *x* number of products produced per month; manage *x* number of people in accomplishing *y* tasks; etc.). Every successful small business should have its basic business metrics and key measures. That's the easy, important part.

But you may not have a strong sense about the critical soft skills you should expect from employees. If that's the case, don't worry. Part II shows you exactly how to define key knowledge, skills, and PEAs. Getting the best out of your superstars means expecting and measuring all critical success factors.

With all of the necessary elements for success in a particular position, you can draft the position description. No doubt you're going to receive lots of resumes. Some of the senders will be qualified, but many won't. You can filter many of the nonsense resumes by first requesting a *strategic* cover letter that guarantees the wrong kind of talent will take one giant step back.

Step #2: Require a Strategic Cover Letter

I'm sure you've noticed duds who are mass-blasting resumes to any company with an open position, regardless of their qualifications. Requiring a strategic cover letter can help sidestep the duds. When you publicize your description of the position, request a cover letter that requires candidates to research your company. Ask two or three open-ended questions that would require candidates to dig into your website or otherwise research your organization.

Here are a few examples of good strategic cover letter questions:

- How do you see yourself relating to our core values? Why?
- What is it about our history that you most identify with? Why?
- Which of our products are you most excited about? Why?

Unlike a resume, a strategic cover letter addresses questions specific to your organization that will most likely deter lazy job-hunters. It would also be your first look at a potential hire's attention to detail, communication skills, and flexibility. Lynette Le Mere, CEO of Pure Joy Catering in Santa Barbara (www.purejoycatering.com), requests strategic cover letters for every position and finds that many candidates "use text with lowercase and no punctuation. It's just terrible."

Some candidates figure words are spelled correctly if no little red lines appear under their words while they were typing in the Word program. That is obviously not always true, but the point here isn't about correct spelling. It's about attention to detail. Even if their writing skills are less than stellar, true superstars will find proofreaders to help them out.

A strategic cover letter can weed out 30 percent of the potential candidates who just won't invest the extra effort to respond. Of those who actually do respond, up to 30 to 40 percent will probably disqualify themselves with incorrect grammar and poor attention to detail, such as not answering your strategic questions. That could leave you with only the top 30 percent to consider for the next phase of your job hunt.

Step #3: Assemble a Hiring Panel

Now, what if you happen to be a CEO who doesn't have access to a panel of superstars virtually or in person? You might consider asking a few of your most trusted vendors, suppliers, and contractors for their confidential assistance in your hiring process. Try bartering their time in exchange for increased use of their services. This way you could potentially get free consulting from experts who really know what it takes to be successful in your industry. I've also seen SBOs contract management consulting companies for their temporary and confidential assistance with their hiring process.

You might also try a staffing agency, but not in the way you probably are thinking. The traditional staffing agency helps find you the right employee. Many staffing agencies offer services you may not have considered before.

Some staffing agencies can actually serve as a *confidential panel* in your hiring process (should you want to keep the search private). Good agencies can offer expert interviewers and help you focus your position description, PEAs, and cover letter questions. You can download the interview I did with Judy Lawton, CEO of The Lawton Group (www.lawtongrp.com). More about Judy later, but her company represents the best in staffing solutions.

Step #4: Dig into the Resumes

Now it's time to dig into the resumes to invite potential hires in for an interview. Divvy up sets of the remaining resumes along with your requirements for the position. Have the panel members take a week or so to pick their top five preferences and prepare a little blurb or two on why they chose their candidates. Many SBOs remove names from resumes just to avoid the potential bias of reviewers in the racking and stacking process.

However you decide to do it, just give your panel enough time to reflect on who they feel would make a great fit. Be sure to define the "why" as well. That can help crystallize position requirements and clues about your culture. Then get the panel back together to review the blurbs and tally the votes for all potential hires. Hash out some kind of consensus on the top few candidates to bring in for an interview.

Step #5: Win the Interview

Consider the interview war. You win by acquiring the right kind of superstar. You also win by inviting the wrong kind of superstar to look elsewhere. You lose by keeping the wrong superstar. You also lose by not being attractive enough as an employer to snag the right kind of talent. You can turn that particular kind of a loss into a win, if you can find out why the superstars turned your position down.

Rally the panel and conduct the interviews. Encourage the panel to agree in advance which questions will be asked of all interviewees and stick firmly to them. Straying from your pre-determined questions can skew the dynamics of each interview and introduces the potential for rabbit holes and interviewee bias. Take yourself and your panel members out of the interviewing process as much as possible. That way you have the luxury of responding primarily to the dynamics the interviewee created.

I'll never forget the time I had to drive up to Los Angeles to interview with a *Fortune 100* company. I was being screened as a potential delivery member for the rollout of their nationwide leadership development program. During the interview, I had to present a 10-minute "training" to a panel of four stone-faced human resource professionals. They literally sat there like ghosts, very deliberately giving me zero interaction and nonverbal feedback.

That was a pretty unrealistic experience. I understand that they were trying to create a hostile environment to see how I'd react. In doing so, however, they created an unrealistic context that I would never encounter when delivering the seminars. Don't do what they did. You don't have to make the interview an unrealistic, sterile experience; just keep it consistent, so you have fewer variables to think about when selecting the best fit.

Immediately after each interview, panel members need to take the time individually to record their thoughts and numerically rate each interviewee. If you or the panel members run right off to the next activity without accomplishing this, you'll likely forget noteworthy subtleties that might have been the difference maker. Reconvene the panel immediately after everyone has had some time for individual assessments.

> **QUESTIONS FOR THE PANEL TO CONSIDER BEFORE THE INTERVIEW**
>
> - What questions will we ask? Will we deviate? If so, how?
> - Will there be any open discussion time? How long?
> - Do our questions cover all the knowledge, skills, and PEAs we need?
> - Will we tally up the results immediately after—or meet back up? If so, when?

Get back together, tally up the thoughts on the respective candidates, and combine comments and ratings on a "Jane Doe for Chief Basket Weaver Position" scorecard. Share "scribe" responsibilities per position (not interviewee), just as someone might take minutes for a meeting. The reason for not sharing scribing duties between interviewees is because different writing styles may influence panel members in different ways. Feel free to offer time for open questions. Just try to eliminate as much of the panel-related variables as possible.

Scorecards can help you to split hairs in competitive hiring situations and focus your check-in conversations.

Step #6: 90-Day Check-In

The rest of this book is about handling everything that will occur in between the hire date and the 30-, 60-, and 90-day check-ins. Part II of this book is all about creating and expecting a consistent message. Part III is about measuring those things using a tailored performance management process. I just wanted to mention the importance of following up right away with all your new hires to benefit from their top-of-mind thoughts on your processes.

Check in with your new hire after 90 days of employment specifically about their overall new-hire experience. That's usually enough time for you to have a good sense of an employee's overall capability and work ethic. The 90-day check-in is your first chance to offer your new hires feedback directly related to *all* the key skills you hired them to deliver.

Pull out the job description and offer specific examples of how they are hitting the *right* target—or missing it, as the case may be.

Be sure to ask how you can better support the employee in doing her job. Ask for feedback on her initial experiences and on your functional processes. There's nobody better to help you see your process inefficiencies than qualified new folks, so take advantage of their fresh perspectives about your organization. They may have great feedback on needlessly complicated internal and external processes.

The best SBOs consistently seek multidirectional feedback—especially from competent, trusted team members. If your team members are not competent and trusted, they shouldn't be there. If they are competent, listen twice as much as you talk. Why else would you have two ears and only one mouth?

At the end of every chapter in this book, you will find a chapter summary checklist. They are meant to offer you a scorecard on the key concepts discussed in the chapter. Read the statements, rate yourself on them, and use the bottom "action" section to list a few actions you can take right now. Then, ask your team members (when it makes sense) to respond to the statements as well, so you can all discuss gaps and decide how, where, and when to improve internal processes.

If the summary questions need to be modified, based on your unique culture—tailor away! You can download a free, fully editable, soft copy of every summary checklist and form in this book from www.christophermcintyre.com. My intent for this book is simply to ask some of the right questions to get you moving in the right direction—not to be the end-all be-all solution for your business.

The collection of chapter summary checklists should offer you a clear framework for *Connecting People to Your Core Message*, and will ultimately install the foundation for . . . your *Roadmap to Freedom!*

Figure 1.4—Chapter 1 Summary Checklist: Attract Superstars

OUTCOME	RATING
Strongly Agree	6
Agree	5
Somewhat Agree	4
Somewhat Disagree	3
Disagree	2
Strongly Disagree	1
KEY STATEMENTS	**RATING**
Checkpoint #1: I ask for all the skills our business needs.	
a. I am clear on the traditional metrics that measure success for every position (knowledge and technical skills).	
b. I am also clear about the PEAs (people skills, work ethic, and attributes) necessary for success in every position.	
c. I communicate and measure those PEAs to maintain our unique business culture.	
d. I ensure that all key skills have been articulated in our position descriptions.	
e. I am prepared to find new superstars.	
Checkpoint #2: I have high-caliber talent begging to work with us.	
a. I have an excellent network that I leverage with two degrees of separation.	
b. I loiter around professional organizations, vendors, and suppliers.	
c. I constantly overbook like the airlines do—even if I'm not hiring.	
d. I have a ready list of folks who have "WOW'd" me.	
e. I know where to find pre- and post-credentialed superstars.	
Checkpoint #3: I have a rock-solid hiring process that weeds out duds.	
a. I use "research us" oriented questions in our strategic cover letter to help weed out the duds.	
b. I have built deliberate redundance in our interviewing process.	
c. I have a panel of superstars ready to help me hire more superstars.	
d. I make sure we "win" every interview even if I lose.	
e. I take full advantage of our new hire's perspectives on our internal process.	

Figure 1.4—**Chapter 1 Summary Checklist: Attract Superstars,** continued

Actions I can take to attract more superstars:
a.
b.
c.
d.
e.

Chapter 2

How to Keep Superstars

A big part of building a "dream team" is to install a systematic process to get the right kind of superstars on board. You've also got to keep any superstars you find—and all the high performers you currently have—on board. Most studies suggest that the top 20 percent of your people give you 80 percent of your most meaningful productivity. Could you imagine what life would be like if you lost ALL of your very best employees—all at once? Talk about a nightmare!

This chapter will focuses more on building core processes that engage, empower, and maximize multidirectional feedback from your superstars.

Delegation for Control Freaks

Employee turnover costs employers roughly two times the individual's annual salary (according to statistics cited on www.salary.com). Given all the time, energy, and resources invested in finding superstars, you may as well keep them on board, right? And, because they're going to be on the team for a while, it makes sense to fully tap into their potential while lightening your workload. Unfortunately, many SBOs fear delegating key tasks to their team—often for good reasons.

The "If Only There Were More of ME" Syndrome

Think about it. You jumped out and created your business. You had the vision. You got things moving. Your choices and intuitive hunches have been consistently rewarded with solid growth. You made things happen. You trust yourself the most. Over the years, perhaps you have encountered many team members who disappointed you: Perhaps they couldn't do the job the way you needed it to be done, had lazy work habits, resisted your authority, or even betrayed you in some fashion. If everyone in your business were half as productive and devoted to your business as you are, life would be grand—wouldn't it?

The problem is, if you don't learn to effectively delegate, your business is limited to your individual bandwidth. And unfortunately, your individual bandwidth won't be enough. You can only make so many phone calls. You can only deal with so many customers. To make matters worse, if what you delegate isn't meaningful, your true superstars will get bored and find meaningful work elsewhere. This is one fundamental way SBOs lose superstars: They make them feel like they are not trusted.

If you're like most SBOs, you probably haven't had the freedom of time to craft a detailed policy manual extracting all the magical processes firmly planted deep within your cranium. So, you've probably just communicated verbally, over and over again, about how you'd like things to be done. However, about 70 percent of spoken words are ignored, misunderstood, or forgotten, according to a 2010 report by the Customer Service Academy. If you don't have written people processes, chances are good that you've been frustrated with individuals who just didn't get it.

Think about the relationship between parents and children for a minute. Every child has to peel away from and find personal meaning in the wisdom parents have imparted. In some cases, they mimic identical behaviors and communication styles. In other cases, they modify or completely disregard the "wisdom" offered. So, too, must your team siphon your wisdom and extract processes to be mimicked—or, in some cases, changed completely.

Your inner control freak may get a little cranky precisely at that "changed completely" moment. But embracing this peeling process can help you keep your superstars because they want to be empowered with work that matters and helps them feel effective. The peeling process also lays a healthy foundation for your future business growth and maximizes your peace of mind because you'll trust that you don't have to do it all.

Chief Distraction Objectifier

Have you ever actually quantified the cost of being too slow to delegate? Try using the Chief Distraction Objectifier tool in Figure 2.1 to answer that qustion.

Figure 2.1—**Chief Distraction Objectifier (Blank)**

Let's start the delegation conversation by defining what you need to get off your plate. Then, let's get you motivated to delegate (more) by looking at how much money you're losing by having to consistently eat from that plate.

Doing ______________________ is a time-wasting task that consistently distracts me from ______________________ (something more important).

I typically deal with ________________________ (time wasting task) wasting _____ hours a day (or week) which equals _____ hours (days) a month.

If I had those____ hours per month to devote to ________________ (more important task) I could probably generate _______ more in revenue (time, resources, focus...) per month, which would equal about _____________ per year.

Figure 2.2 gives you an example of how you can use it. Let's apply the example to a common distraction, like email.

Figure 2.2—"Chief Distraction Objectifier" Email Example

> Getting wrapped up in low-priority emails is a time-wasting task that consistently distracts me from connecting with priority leads (something more important).
>
> I typically deal with email (time-wasting task) three hours a day, which equals 60 hours a month (3 hours / day x 5 days per week = 15 hours per week, 60 hours per month).
>
> If I had those 60 hours per month to invest in quality leads (more important task) I could probably generate two more accounts in revenue per month, which would equal about $1.2 million per year.

Yes, you have to deal with email. But how much time do you *waste* constantly checking email? Most busy professionals waste about three hours per day dealing with unimportant emails.

Maybe your issue isn't email. Maybe it's dealing with customers. Maybe it's creating spreadsheets for a dud on your team. Maybe it's drafting proposals because you're the only one you really trust to estimate bids correctly. You get the idea. Find issues to run through the objectifier and prioritize those you want to address.

Aside from the direct costs you could be saving by delegating more, what about the indirect benefits?

- Spending more time with family?
- Getting better sleep at night because you trust your team with more?
- Feeling better about business in general?
- Reaping the rewards of consistently using your strengths in the right areas?
- Being better prepared to see the "big picture" because you're less engulfed by the busy-trap?

Objectify the cost of consistently doing the things *least* worthy of your attention. Now, add that to the cost of not doing the things *most* worthy of your attention. That should help to get you motivated enough to delegate more tasks right away.

Three Levels of Delegation

Some SBOs can be control freaks with impossibly high standards. If that's you, the first step is to admit you have a problem. Some SBOs like delegating but don't trust the individuals they're delegating to. Either way, it's OK to start slow. There are three degrees of delegation: micro-manage, responsibility, authority.

Level I of Delegation: Micromanage

Depending on the depth of your addiction to doing everything yourself, you may need serious work just learning to exercise your delegation muscle. Let's define "addiction" as anything you consistently do that's not good for you. We all have addictions to something–what's yours? It's OK to start small by delegating, and micro-managing, addictive tasks of maximum *insignificance*.

Define what, when, and how it should be done and then watch it happen or check in frequently. I've seen many SBOs ask delegates to objectify a particular process before beginning. You could also ask your delegates to draw up the plan they intend to take, step by step. In this way, you could actually have your delegates create their position's functional manual. By having delegates bring you their version of a process, you're able to check for gaps in their understanding and then you may be forced to consider fresh ways of handling a particular task.

Level II and III of Delegation: Responsibility and Authority

A big piece of keeping superstars hinges on being able to delegate responsibility and authority for important work. Here you are imparting varying degrees of responsibility and authority for task accomplishment.

At Level II and III, you can be less concerned about *how* things get done, but you still want to be crystal clear about *what* you expect and *when* you expect it.

How fantastic would work be if you weren't necessary for your business's success? Now, you might think: "I love what I do, and I want to be necessary." I understand that perspective. I just want to point out that there is a huge productivity difference between working in your business because you *want to* and because you *have to*.

When you work because you *want to*, you're enabling yourself to show up with less tension and more presence and energy. When you work because you *have to*, you'll be more likely to show up with contagious negative stress even before the day begins. You'll probably be less willing to delegate the important work that feeds superstar longevity.

Be prepared to fully delegate everything. The less necessary you are, the more empowered you are to *work on* the business instead of constantly *working in* the business (*E-Myth Unabridged*, by Michael Gerber, 2004). When you choose to work in the business (i.e., making the pies, writing the code, planning the event), you're doing so simply because you want to. In this way you can be more in control. Ironically, getting more control happens by *letting go of more control.* The key to maximizing trust, while letting go of control, lies in unpacking accountability.

Four Elements for Owning Accountability

My favorite book suggests: "Faith, if it hath not works, is dead" (KJV Bible, James 2:17). To me, that means if you believe in something, it is senseless unless you back it up with appropriate actions. Similarly, delegation without accountability backing it up is also meaningless. You can better empower your superstars by clarifying all four elements of accountability:

1. Why is the task important?

2. Who owns the task?
3. What does "done" look like?
4. Who owns the process?

Answering these four questions will clarify the importance, responsibility, and authority for any delegated task. It will also help you identify developmental needs for you and your team (see Figure 2.3). Failure to hold superstars accountable for inadequate results is unacceptable.

Figure 2.3—**Installing Accountability and Ownership**

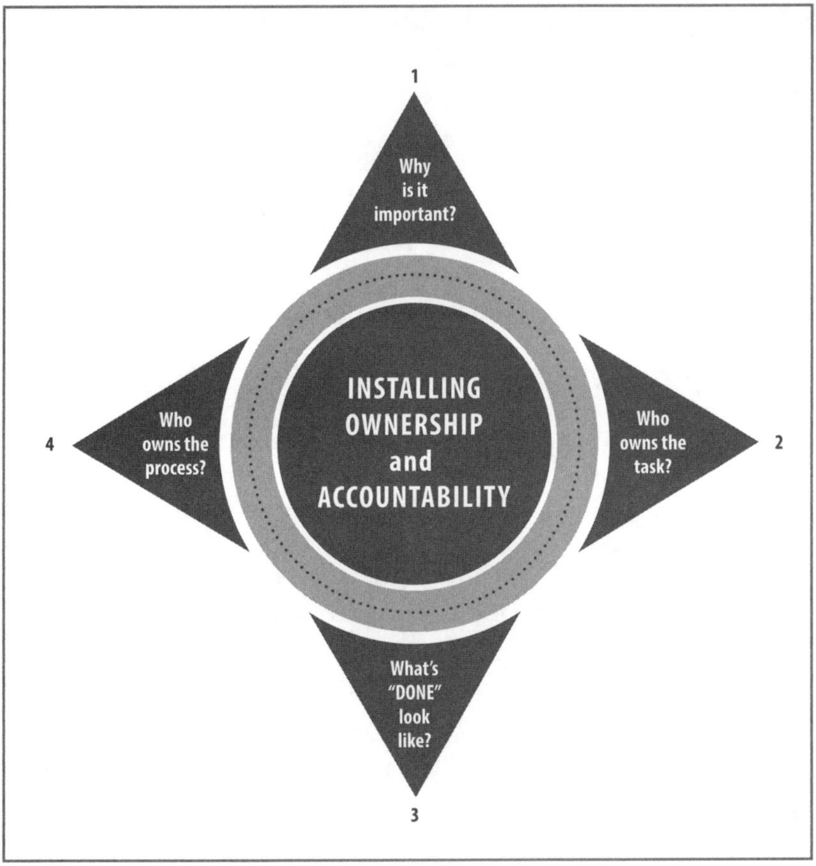

Delegating tasks without unpacking accountability is kind of like wishing someone well on an aimless journey through the wilderness. Who does that? SBOs who are too busy to clarify their work. The challenge sometimes, though, is that a lack of clarity on the front end of delegation can create more problems downstream. Your anticipating problems downstream may be hindering your willingness to delegate. Installing accountability can minimize the potential for problems.

Why Is the Task Important?

Start by defining why the task is necessary in the first place. If it's not valuable, why do it, right? If delegates are not clear as to why tasks are being delegated, they may classify the jobs a low priority or ignore your request.

- Why is it necessary for your business?
- What business goal is it tied to?
- How is this task supporting your key customers, products, or services?
- How is the task contributing to the bottom line?

To the extent possible, provide as much context for *why* the task is necessary in order to save you time in the long run. Superstars want to know that the task means something.

Who Owns the Task?

With the strategic *why* in mind, pick the best owner for the task. Having a genuine reason for why you chose someone to run with a task communicates deliberate leadership to your team. You know your team best, so choose wisely. Random delegation is lazy leadership that will ultimately damage your brand and create even more people problems.

Once you've assigned the task, have your superstar acknowledge responsibility. You could actually ask, "OK, so do you have it?" It may seem like overengineering the process, but I can't count how many times I've watched SBOs never "officially" hand off a task. Instead, they talk around it or invite "anyone" to think about it when what they really wanted was for someone specific to do something specific.

Make sure your team knows the difference between you brainstorming ideas with the group and when you are actually delegating work. Every project or subproject must have one clear owner.

What Does "Done" Look Like?

With the *why* (value) and the *who* (owner) established, it's now time for a clear agreement as to *what* should actually be accomplished. What, specifically, is the desired outcome? What does "done" look like? The trick is getting the outcome to be clear in the mind of the employee assigned the task.

<u>These questions can help point to clear outcomes:</u>

- At what point is this particular issue done and off my radar?
- How exactly will I objectively measure the outcome?
- What does "the wrong way" look like?
- What's better or different after task completion?

Here is an example of how easily miscommunication gaps can happen. What if you tell an employee you want your customer service processes improved? That seems pretty simple, right? You have an idea of what that means, and so does your employee.

So your employee marches off to improve your website. In his mind, improving the website means creating an entirely new website to improve customer experience. But this task wasn't what you had in mind at all: You simply wanted to improve handling of customer complaints about product delivery.

When that kind of miscommunication occurs, arguments ensue, trust is lost, and no one wins. You're frustrated because the employee should have known what you meant (especially since you were just talking about the product errors). Your superstar is angry because he did exactly what you told him, yet you never seem to be satisfied.

Meanwhile, the problem still exists: Customers are walking away because your company is consistently sending the wrong products.

This kind of gap can also lead to the "If you want it done right, you just need to do it yourself" mentality. So, you decide to take on the project yourself and spend the next two months untangling the issues. Meanwhile, the rest of your work is building up, and you're becoming the bottleneck for more important issues. Your employees are growing more frustrated every day because you have taken on all the meaningful projects and they're not getting the important work. The employee who had the assignment stripped away from him becomes particularly upset and resentful watching you perform the task he had been assigned.

> **POP QUIZ**
>
> When was the last time you thought: If you want something done right, you've got to do it yourself?

You see where this self-created black hole is going, right? As they say in the military: "What we've got here is a good, old-fashioned soup sandwich." This may have happened in part because you weren't as clear as you could have been about your desired results. Not clearly identifying specific results is much like trying to eat a soup sandwich with your hands. It's messy and probably spilling all over the place.

Who Owns the Process?

The last element when installing accountability is to clarify who owns the process. This doesn't mean micromanaging the process. You just need to get everyone in agreement about who is in charge of deciding "how" the assignment will get done. In this way, you will minimize any confusion about who has the authority to make certain decisions.

There may be times when it's not possible for you to be clear on what the process will be. If this is the case, have the employee draft her suggestions on how best to handle the process. That will give you something to objectively discuss, agree on, and document when you have a status update discussion.

However it happens, clarify and distinguish between the task (who) and process (how) owner. Document it all in writing whenever appropriate. That documentation will come in handy later, in Part III, when we look at your performance conversation system.

Here's how an imaginary conversation between SBO (Mary) and delegate (Ben) should go down.

Mary: Hey, Ben, do you have a minute?

Ben: Sure, Mary, what's up?

Mary: You remember we set that goal of getting customer service complaints down to 2 percent this year, right?

Ben: Yeah, I remember that. We're going to do it, too.

Mary: Agreed. We've got an issue though. Eli in shipping just gave me the quarterly numbers, and it looks like we've actually seen a 10 percent increase in complaints this quarter. It seems our customers are getting the Flux Capacitors instead of the Pez Dispensers. Obviously, our customer service numbers are moving in the wrong direction, and, if it keeps happening, we're going to start losing key customers.

Ben: Oh, wow. That's weird. Do you want me to take a look at our customer service initiatives?

Mary: Yes. You're the best at dealing with angry customers, and no one knows the shipping processes like you do. Please find out why we're having the recent increase in shipping errors and fix the issues. Could you also put a plan together for dealing with the customers already impacted and let me know the best way to compensate them before you roll it out? Try to get on my calendar by Friday and let me know what you came up with.

Ben: No problem, Mary.

Mary: OK, just so we're speaking the same language here: Can you confirm the agreements we've just made?

(Mary puts a reminder that she expects to hear from Ben, re: Pez issues next Friday on her calendar.)

Ben: Yep. I'm going to untangle and fix the recent increase in customer complaints about receiving the Flux Capacitors instead of the Pez dispensers. I'm also going to figure out how to best compensate the folks already impacted by the errors. I'll track you down on Friday with an update and the plan, right?

(Ben writes the task onto his To Do list).

Mary: You got it. Good thing we read this part of Chris's book, huh?

Ben *(thinks to himself)***:** Oh, yeah. If it weren't for his book, you probably would have just done it all by yourself like you always do, you control freak.

Mary *(thinks to herself)*: Hmmm . . . what else can I give Ben?

In the above scenario, you see all four elements of installed accountability in action. Mary defined why the task was important (increased customer service complaints). She strategically chose an owner (Ben) because he was the best with disgruntled customers and knew the shipping process well. She delegated full authority in one area (fix the issues) and partial authority in another area (plan to reimburse the customers). She included the safeguard of having the process signed off on prior to rollout. In this instance, Mary used a deadline and also checked for understanding just to make sure she hadn't miscommunicated the desired outcome.

Life is good when customers get their Pez dispensers, so get caught following up. If a task is important enough to delegate, it should be important enough to notice when it's finished. If you're not tracking your important pending tasks (or "waiting fors"), you may not be in complete control of your work.

Mary could track her *waiting for* list like this:

- Ben—Pez Issues and Reimbursement Plan since October 4 (due October 10th)
- Ben—statistics on customer service complaints (since October 2nd)

If you delegate and never notice what's been done, sooner or later your delegates will stop paying attention to the things you've assigned. Not because they mean to ignore you; they just don't believe you think the work is important enough to notice. Just remember, if it's not a priority for you, it probably won't be for your team. Plug in your own real-life example here, but the important thing is to be clear about agreements, accountability, authority, and following up.

Install Multidirectional Feedback Systems

Now that your superstars have clear parameters and space to run with important work, I challenge you to humble yourself and install what I call *multidirectional feedback systems*. This means that you need to bake candid feedback into everything you—and your superstars—do. I say "humble" because one of the best ways to get your superstars to own their mistakes is for you to consistently own yours. Here are some simple ways you can do that.

Multidirectional Feedback: Embrace the Opportunity to Suck

It's tough to be the chief, huh? On one hand, you've got to have answers to issues you don't even understand. On the other, your team is well aware when you have no clue about what you've said or done wrong. As chief, you have to walk the slippery slope of being competent enough to follow yet competent enough to admit when you're confused, make a mistake, or forget something.

A simple way to keep your superstars is to be honest when you suck at something. Have fun with it. You may as well admit when you're struggling or are not sure about what you're doing. Your team notices your mistakes and shortcomings just as clearly as you identify theirs.

Your willingness to admit your struggles empowers your team to step up and be of more use. Remember that concept? It also encourages them to feel safe enough to admit their weaknesses, too. When you recognize and readily admit what things you suck at, you'll be more open to opportunities for improvement. What a great company value: *Embrace the opportunity to suck.*

Multidirectional Feedback: Get Caught Being Wrong

As an SBO, your business relies on you to consistently have the right answers. Lucky for you, you probably are right most of the time. The challenge with being right so much is that you also must recognize when you're wrong. One way to speed this up is with an Argument Audit. For fun, try filling out the second row in Figure 2.4 using details from your last disagreement with an employee.

Figure 2.4—**Argument Audit**

ARGUMENT AUDIT					
Date	**Who**	**Issue**	**I Said**	**They Said**	**Verdict**
Feb. 12	Wayne	Customer database wasn't being updated in a timely manner	We need that info quickly to improve customer service the next time they call	The database is confusing, and too busy so it's overwhelming	We went with Wayne's suggestion to appoint rotating database duties weekly

The danger of always being right (even if you really are) is that you're setting yourself up to constantly have all the answers for your team, which indirectly encourages less genuine input from your team. Decreased superstar involvement leads to their underemployment and dissatisfaction, and ultimately more burnout and less freedom for you. Be wrong more often or budget for the costs of always being right.

Multidirectional Feedback: Write Out the Unwritten Rules

One final way to keep superstars genuinely engaged is to address the unwritten rules. There are unwritten rules in every organization (yes, even yours). Of course, no one ever formally recognizes them even though everyone knows they're there. Accept that you have these rules and write them out with your team. Then you can either live by them or try address some of them.

I'll give you a personal example of an unwritten rule. When I was in the Air Force, my primary role was as the Wing Deployment Officer. I was responsible for the logistics required to deploy the entire Wing. It seemed like a pretty big job, but I quickly realized I wasn't really "leading" much of anything. While responsible, I didn't have much authority. Remember that fourth element of installed accountability?

There was a clear, though unwritten rule in place that put the pilots above the agreed-upon processes. In fact, when I first came to the office my boss put a sign on my office door: "Lt. McIntyre, OIC, BOHICA." That meant Lt. McIntyre (me) was Officer in Charge (OIC) of the "Bend Over Here It Comes Again" (BOHICA) flight. That was my welcome to Air Force life–and its unwritten rules.

I found that most of my responsibility was in chasing the whims of ego-heavy fighter pilots. As you might imagine, there were tons of rules, regulations, and other safety processes that needed to be followed while moving people and sensitive equipment. But in the ultra-fast, type-A personality world of a fighter pilot, there's really only one way to do things–the pilot's way. Managing logistics was particularly difficult

TRY ASKING YOUR SUPERSTARS THESE QUESTIONS ABOUT WRITTEN RULES

- What written rules do we violate?
- What unwritten rules do we have?
- When was the last time you saw it in place?
- What can we do to address it?
- If we can't stop it, is there any way we can make it easier to deal with?

when pilots frequently did whatever they wanted and expected the logistics team to clean up their dust.

The job was difficult because of the unwritten rule: "If you're not a fighter pilot, you're a second-class citizen." Of course, that rule was never officially communicated; in fact, it was publicly denied. The people in command consistently communicated that the Wing Deployment Officer called the logistics shots, but it simply wasn't true.

Now don't get me wrong. The primary role of the Air Force is to provide air support. I get that. If the official rule had been something like "Shut up and cater to the whims of fighter pilots," then I would have known my place. But the official rule was that the Wing Deployment Office owned the logistics process; that's what made the unwritten rule favoring fighter pilots so difficult to accept.

As an SBO—unlike many of your corporate counterparts—you have the unique opportunity to lay the foundation for an organization free from unnecessary politics and unwritten rules. Addressing unwritten rules can earn you the respect of your superstars because at least they'll know you have the integrity to try.

The bottom line is that you need to write out the unwritten rules and then deliberately play by them—or risk seeing your superstars fly away.

Figure 2.5—Chapter 2 Summary Checklist: Keep Superstars

OUTCOME	RATING
Strongly Agree	6
Agree	5
Somewhat Agree	4
Somewhat Disagree	3
Disagree	2
Strongly Disagree	1
KEY STATEMENTS	**RATING**
Checkpoint #1: I can fully delegate most of my important work.	
a. I've objectified the costs of my biggest time wasters.	
b. I am motivated to delegate as much as possible.	
c. I comfortably could delegate everything if I needed to.	
d. I distinguish between the three levels of delegation.	
e. I actively pursue level-three delegation with all of my direct reports.	
Checkpoint #2: I trust and empower my team.	
a. I never delegate without installing accountability.	
b. I always define the impact a task will have on objectives and goals.	
c. I don't just divvy up work evenly among my team; delegation happens strategically.	
d. I always articulate the clear end result I expect.	
e. I always decide who will own the process along the way.	
Checkpoint #3: I've installed multidirectional feedback systems.	
a. I refuse to have all the answers.	
b. I embrace the opportunity to suck.	
c. I make sure I get caught being wrong.	
d. I consistently check for and actively deal with unwritten rules.	
e. My team is comfortable calling me out when I'm wrong.	

Figure 2.5—Chapter 2 Summary Checklist: Keep Superstars, continued

Actions I could take to keep my superstars:
a.
b.
c.
d.
e.

Chapter 3

How to Lose Nightmares

Attracting Superstars? Check. Keeping Superstars? Check. Before we get into how to offer your superstars a consistent message, there's one last puzzle piece necessary for systematically crafting the right team: learning to drop nightmare employees like hot rocks.

Now to be fair, even cancer can be treated. So when it comes to letting someone go, it should be obvious that it *had* to happen and was a last resort. Generally speaking, you should not fire anyone until consistent and very specific documented feedback concerning any problem has been offered. The more you can show an employee has been given guidance on how to resolve their issues, the better.

But let's face it: There just comes a point when it's time to let someone go. You may not be facing that time right now, but this chapter will help you when that time does come.

Most organizations have nightmare employees. A nightmare employee represents a consistent *hitch in your get-along*. Maybe he started off as a shining star and then spiraled down from the sky. Maybe she's holding you hostage because she's an integral part of your business and you fear losing her critical skills. He might have many friends in the office, and you worry about how firing him will impact morale. She may be your friend or—even worse—a family member.

Regardless of your rationalization of the problem, chances are the nightmare probably should've been ejected long ago. Have you ever considered the real cost of allowing nightmares to continue to spew their toxic funk around you and your team?

How much are your nightmares costing you?

- How much peace of mind have you wasted thinking about firing that person?
- How many bad days has this individual inflicted on your superstars?
- How many times have your superstars resented you for not doing your job and getting rid of the nightmare?

Nightmare personnel also impact you in an invisible way, much like depression. It's tougher to get up in the morning. The days seem longer and less productive. Important issues don't receive the focus and thinking they require. Once the nightmare (and depression) is gone, the funk begins to lift, and the days begin to seem brighter.

Unfortunately, it could take years to really recover mentally—and sometimes financially—from the negative impact of your nightmare. That said, let's review how to drop your nightmares.

Own it: Nightmares Are Always Your Fault

First thing first: As the SBO, you must own responsibility for your nightmare. The nightmares are sitting squarely on your shoulders, draining your energy and demotivating your superstars. If you've got a nightmare on your hands, it's your fault—period. It may not be your fault that they're choosing to underperform, but it is your fault that they're empowered to work their funky magic under your roof. Peter

Drucker, often referred to as the "father of modern management," said it best in his book, *The Profession of Management*:

> *If I put a person in a job and he or she does not perform I have made a mistake. I have no business blaming that person.*

Stop blaming your nightmares for having become what they are. Pointing out slackers under your leadership is really just pointing at your own lack of leadership. You're in charge. My pastor always says, "There are sins of *commission* and then there are sins of *omission*." What he means is that at times we *commit* sin by doing something we know we shouldn't. But there are other times when we sin by not doing (*omitting*) something we should.

Failing to address your nightmares is a sin of omission. You're actually rewarding the nightmares with a second home (your business) to terrorize. You're also punishing your superstars and creating a negative culture that your customers will ultimately feel. The byproduct of your choice is low morale and unnecessary organizational drag. Repent . . . or you'll have a new unwritten rule: *Nightmares welcome here!*

Sometimes You *Are the Nightmare*

Here's a leadership tip: If you seem to frequently attract the wrong kind of talent or can't figure out why superstars always start off as wide-eyed fireballs and quickly end up as demotivated slugs, *you* may be the nightmare. Even with best of intentions, your leadership, or lack thereof, may be inspiring certain employees to become uninspired nightmares.

If you have difficulty retaining talent or seem to always have a few too many nightmares on staff, you might want to consider hiring a chief operating officer or someone better at managing the "people" issues. Depending on your particular struggle, that person might need to be a "bad cop," if you suck at holding folks accountable. Similarly, that person might need to play "good cop" if you suck at giving genuine praise and motivating your team.

Figure 3.1—Where Might "I" be the Nightmare?

I MIGHT JUST BE THE NIGHTMARE	
Possible Example	**Possible Impact**
I gave conflicting information to two separate people.	The team got one message—but our customers get another.
I didn't correct a people problem early on.	Operations and Sales have adopted an "us" vs. "them" mentality—and are blaming each other and not working together.
I "blew up" on my entire team because one person made a mistake.	Everyone tiptoes around me, and no one is willing to get creative anymore.
Other	
Other	

Try filling out Figure 3.1 to help you determine where you might be the nightmare. In doing so, you need to take a good, hard look in the mirror.

Be curious about situations in which you may be creating the nightmare–or in which you are the nightmare yourself. It's OK to admit either scenario. All of us have a little nightmare in us. But by pinpointing specific examples of how you are a nightmare, it will help you avoid creating them on your staff.

Get Fired Up to Fire

Although firing is never pleasant or easy, you need to find ways to get motivated to do it. One way to get motivated is to recognize that you're just stuck in a failing relationship. For those of you who have been through this situation, I'm sure you knew long before you parted ways that the relationship was headed down the drain. You may have delayed the inevitable for a host of reasons.

A superstar can mutate into a nightmare for three common reasons:

1. She has become lazy, entitled, or autocratic.
2. The organization has changed (grown, improved, or shifted focus), but the employee has not.
3. He was never who he said he was in the first place (fancy degrees with zero common sense, phony accolades, fluffy credentials).

Try to find clarity about why the relationship has gone bad. Understanding who or what shifted can help you to provide more useful feedback. It can also help you avoid repeating similar hiring mistakes in the future. The more specific you can be about why someone isn't working out, the more sure you can be about which key soft skills will be most necessary to protect your distinct culture.

It may also be that you're getting exactly what you've requested, but your perception is off about your current culture, mission, or organizational needs. Isn't that how American car companies once lost their competitive edge? They were consistently hitting the bull's-eye on the wrong targets; doing so created systemic cancer. I'm sure I don't have to tell you that cancer spreads through the body if it's not treated immediately. David Stebbins, of the Stebbins Group, phrases it like this:

> *When you have a small office, eventually you consider the people friends, but my needs must come first. $30k to $40k worth of checks go out the door each month, so many people are counting on me. If I don't stay in business and become profitable, a lot of people aren't going to be able to count on that money. So I don't have the right not to fire someone when that person is hindering success. I actually have a responsibility to let him go.*

It's Time to Fire When . . .

One of the key questions SBOs often ask is when to fire someone.

Fire When: Your Gut Says So

The answer inevitably boils down to "trusting your gut." Think back to all the times you've trusted your gut. I'll bet there are minimal instances in which you listened to that gut feeling and ultimately made the wrong call. In my research, I've found that most SBOs waited far too long to listen to their instincts.

Be sure you don't misunderstand my point. I'm not suggesting you fire anyone who looks at you the wrong way and causes some discomfort in your gut. But in most cases, your gut will probably point you in the direction most congruent with your written and unwritten values.

You may be wondering: "What do I do if I'm too close to the situation and no longer trust my ability to make a gut call on this matter?" In this event, perhaps you should build a team of trusted confidants for frequent check-ins. You can make the most of trusted advisors by having clear and objective expectations with well-documented written feedback. The more frequently you document, the less subjectivity you have to get hung up on.

Speaking of documentation, there's another good reason for it. No employer wants to get sued. Documentation will be a vital resource should you ever experience legal challenges about deciding to let someone go. Part III of this book is about creating a tailored performance conversation system that will give you all the specific documentation you may need.

Fire When: You Are Taking Them Home with You

If you and your confidants believe there is nothing else to be done to improve the employee's performance, it's likely time to move to the next step. You will save yourself a great deal of headaches, frustration, and perhaps even shredded vocal cords from constantly repeating yourself to this employee and losing your temper.

Here is one more quick thought about knowing when to let someone go. A good friend of mine, who is also an SBO, said, "When I'm consistently taking them home with me at night, I know it's time to let them go." He meant that if an employee's performance was so bad that he constantly spent time worrying about it—even at home while spending quality with his family—then he knew it was time to let her or him go. Do not let your nightmares haunt you.

Fire When: You Can No Longer Ignore the Costs

One way to find the motivation to let someone go is to try to calculate the cost of keeping someone too long. If you were to go out of business:

- Who would be negatively affected?
- What impact would it have on your family?
- Where would your employees go?
- Would any vendors or suppliers be negatively impacted?
- How would your ability to contribute to your community (or the world) be impacted?

Get fired up enough to act quickly: If you don't fire your nightmares, your customers will! Check out Dave Konstantin's (K-Co Construction's) free interview on my website for a good laugh around the costs of not firing someone soon enough. I heard some amazing and extremely motivating stories while doing the interviews.

> You can download the conversations I had with SBOs interviewed for this book at www.christophermcintyre.com.

You're Fired!

It's inevitable: At some point you're going to have to fire folks. This is really difficult for a variety of reasons. Here are some ways of looking at it, and tactics that may help make this sensitive issue a bit easier.

Put Them Out of Their Misery

You might be surprised to find that most nonperformers are ready to go. No matter who you are, consistently underperforming doesn't feel good. Assuming your nightmare employee isn't psychotic, it's quite possible she feels incompetent from all of the browbeating and warnings. Put her out of her misery. When she wakes up tomorrow, she'll probably feel relieved that she no longer has a job she couldn't perform well. Certain jobs and work environments just aren't meant for some people. Think of this as you assisting your nightmares to find their true purpose at this particular point in time.

Think back to the last time you felt incompetent. Have you ever had a job that you just couldn't do well? I remember being in one such situation when I was in college and working at a Red Lobster. I was horrible. I tend to learn very slowly in positions with a ton of options, variables, and low consistency. If there are no "firm" concepts for me to begin to grasp, I struggle to connect the dots.

While it may sound simple to you, I just couldn't "get it" at Red Lobster. There were so many different combinations of suggested wines with dinner plates. There was an ever-changing menu. Customers would say, "This steak's not rare." Or, they would ask if they could substitute this for that. No matter how quickly I moved, I couldn't quite pick up the rhythm necessary for success in that particular role.

None of the other servers wanted to split a section with me because they knew I'd "be in the weeds" all night. This meant they knew I'd be behind all night, and they'd have to pick up my slack. I was fully expecting to be fired every day and was completely embarrassed. I was miserable and honestly wouldn't have minded being put out of my misery. The only thing that kept me from getting fired was my personality. Most of the employees and customers liked me.

Have you ever kept someone too long because she had one great skill? Try answering the Misery Log in Figure 3.2 on page 51 to determine when you could be quicker to put someone out of their misery.

To be clear: As is often the case, the problem wasn't lack of talent. It's just that I wasn't a talented *server*. If they had fired me, they would have done me a favor. However, if they *had* let me go, I would have had a legitimate legal case because the company didn't have any metrics to prove I was underperforming.

Figure 3.2—**The Misery Log**

KEY QUESTION	EXAMPLE	YOUR TURN
Who is someone I kept too long?	Chris—the server at Red Lobster	
What was the impact?	Lost several key customers, team members don't want to partner with him	
When did I first know I needed to let the person go?	When Jeff (who never complains about anything) told me he really needed to go	
Why didn't I fire that person?	His personality—customers loved him, and he was great for morale of internal team (fun guy)	
How can I keep from repeating the same mistake in the future?	Have quarterly performance conversations that look at entire profile (customer service, cook inputs . . . etc.)	

The Metrics Told You This Was Coming

Measurable metrics are a big piece of a rock-solid performance conversation program (which we will create in Parts II and III). For now, though, give this serious thought. If you had to let someone go today and an external committee had reviewed your choice, what

POP QUIZ

If you had to fire one person on your team today, who would it be and why? Would you be able to pull out a documented paper trail of clear measures consistently not being met? Could you show the person undeniable, objective proof that he or she has consistently hit the wrong targets? If the answer is "no" to the questions above, you might have a noteworthy problem, but one that can be easily fixed: Measure and document more.

documentation would you be able to provide, right now, to validate your case?

To make the metrics challenge even more difficult, what if you had to fire someone based on her people skills alone? Or, how could you document her lack of support for your long-term goals or values? Could you show a committee proof of conversations you've had? Again, if you're like most SBOs, your two-letter answer probably rhymes with "oh!"

If you're thinking "No, I don't have the documentation now, but I could create it quickly," chances are you'd only focus on the most recent examples. Can you provide documented proof of themes and trends throughout the employee's entire employment history? Your long-term freedom requires it.

To put it simply, you need to be able prove that *you* aren't the nightmare—which is exactly what world-class nightmare employees will claim. In that way, having the right metrics can keep you out of court and put an end to your misery. The quarterly conversation process and form, in Part III, will give you all the metrics you need. More on that soon.

Don't Apologize

Let's assume that you've taken responsibility for letting nightmares go when it's time. You have been keeping solid documentation with tons of specific feedback, and you're finally ready to have the tough conversation! At this point, the termination conversation should not in any way be about the big, bad, bully boss firing an innocent, unassuming employee. It's simply about delivering the consequences ordered by an *employee* who has consistently failed to meet clearly communicated expectations. You're just delivering the message they've earned, kind of like a postman delivers mail.

Don't apologize for having to fire—just deliver the mail.

If that is the case, what legitimate reason do you have to apologize? There isn't one. Apologizing makes it sound like you are to blame for the employee's performance, which is not the case. Don't give any room to allow the conversation to slip into a mud-slinging contest.

Figure 3.3 provides ten more dos and don'ts to consider when firing employee nightmares.

Figure 3.3—**Ten Dos and Don'ts When Firing Nightmares**

DO	DON'T
1. Be familiar with unemployment laws (and have appropriate documentation)	1. Argue
2. Draft responses for questions the individual may ask	2. Offer advice
3. Prepare in advance how to divvy up workload	3. Leak your plans to others (unless they will be in the room)
4. Plan the day and time (if possible)	4. Procrastinate
5. Have someone else in the room	5. Take responsibility for the failure
6. Focus on the performance (not the person)	6. Focus on the person
7. Be respectful	7. Do it in public
8. Give the person space to share their thoughts / feelings	8. Talk about your own feelings
9. Be specific about what will happen next (pay, benefits, unused vacation, etc.)	9. Defend yourself or your decision
10. Keep it quick (10–15 minutes max)	10. Babble or try to break the ice

Here are some words that you can tailor to get you going into the tough discussion:

> *Randy, after reviewing your work performance for this quarter, we concluded that this job is not a good fit for your skills. Because of that, today is your last day. I am sure you have a lot on your mind, but are there any issues or questions you feel you want to share or discuss with me at this time? You will have time to gather your personal items, and Lisa can assist you.*

One way to allow someone to save face is to offer him the opportunity to resign. In that way, he can move on to other employment opportunities without having the stigma of being "fired." That may give you some wiggle room to offer your nightmare a more positive way out, if that's something you would prefer.

You both did your best, but it isn't working out at this particular period in time. The business needs a change. There–you just did it!

Just Did It

I'm sure you're familiar with Nike's slogan: *Just Do It*. Well, how about *Just Did It* instead? That could be your phrase for when you've decided someone needs to go.

Trust yourself. Don't procrastinate. There comes a point where the thinking is done, and the action needs to begin. Continuing to ruminate about your decision to finally fire your nightmare costs you time and energy and robs your team of mental resources and morale. Don't continue to allow nightmares to haunt your soul. Just Did It.

As the SBO, your role is to ensure your business goals are being met. When someone consistently fails to contribute to the strategic direction of the business, whether because of a lack of skill or some other reason, you must remember that you are fulfilling your role when you let that person go. It may not be easy, but, in the end, everyone ultimately benefits from getting rid of nightmares that won't support your consistent message.

Speaking of a consistent message—what's yours? I mean, aside from "what" you expect (improved metrics, increased sales, multiple deliverables), what success formula will consistently show everyone "how" to live your brand? Part II, *Create Your Core Mantra*, will show you exactly how to create, clarify, and systematically expect a consistent core message that's right for you, your team, and your most valuable assets.

Figure 3.4—Chapter 3 Summary Checklist: How to Lose Nightmares

OUTCOME	RATING
Strongly Agree	6
Agree	5
Somewhat Agree	4
Somewhat Disagree	3
Disagree	2
Strongly Disagree	1
KEY STATEMENTS	**RATING**
Checkpoint #1: I realize my "nightmares" are my fault.	
a. I have no nightmares on my team.	
b. I don't blame my nightmares for being nightmares.	
c. I've calculated the costs of the impact nightmares have on me.	
d. I've calculated the costs of the impact nightmares have on my superstars.	
e. I've calculated the costs of the impact nightmares have on my customers, vendors, suppliers, and others that experience our brand.	
Checkpoint #2: I can get motivated to fire when I need to.	
a. I always trust my gut when letting go of nightmares.	
b. I realize nightmares will ultimately feel better somewhere else.	
c. Nightmares are miserable here—and I realize I'm doing them a favor by letting them go.	
d. I realize I don't have the right NOT to fire nightmares.	
e. I realize it's not "me" firing someone—it's "them" not meeting standards.	
Checkpoint #3: I am good at firing my nightmares.	
a. I keep the firing conversation short (10-15 minutes).	
b. I don't argue about my decision.	
c. I have multiple examples of specific feedback around failed objectives.	
d. I never apologize for having to fire someone.	
e. I never fire in public.	

Figure 3.4—**Chapter 3 Summary Checklist: How to Lose Nightmares,** continued

Actions I could take to neutralize or lose my nightmares:
a.
b.
c.
d.
e.

Part II

Create Your Core Mantra

Now that you have a superstar team (and even if you don't), you can improve everyone's performance by creating a more consistent message about how to be successful. Connecting your team to a consistent message is essential to promoting a philosophy that enables the brand of your business.

That said, what is the core message you consistently communicate around *how* results should be achieved in your business? Part II of this book helps you define just that, by:

- Distinguishing between systematic and situational success
- Introducing a "mantra" leadership concept
- Creating a tailored systematic success "formula" to achieve your mantra

After you've defined your core mantra, and developed a distinct formula that enables it, you can *Connect your People to the Core*. If you're absolutely certain your superstars have bought into a consistent message that enables your brand, just skim the content and summary checklists found in Chapters 4 through 8 for useful nuggets and tools. Then jump to *Part III: Install Your Core Mantra* for ideas on how to improve the dialogue you have with superstars about their performance.

If you know you could be better at getting that core message out of your head and firmly into the minds of your superstars—read on.

Chapter 4

Developing a Systematic Success Formula

When I was interviewing SBOs from across the country for this book, a very unexpected thing happened. I noticed, after the fact, that in every interview there was a very distinct key theme, or mantra, each SBO believed in most when it came to leading their teams. They all had a simple, yet uniquely different, approach for inspiring their superstars to consistently achieve their business goals.

What's Your Leadership Mantra?

I never directly asked about a mantra or a succinct formula for success. But in every interview it showed up clearly. In fact, many of the SBOs actually thanked *me* for interviewing them when it was over. It helped them to more clearly see what they've done, where they've come from, and what they most unconsciously believed in. For many, much of their success and their beliefs leading to their success had been previously completely invisible to them.

In many small businesses, there are gaps between performance, effort, and output of the SBO and the employees. Many SBOs have difficulty finding a way to get their team to see, believe in, and embrace the business goals as sincerely as they do. You might expect that, given the increased incentives the SBO has for the business to do well. On the other hand, however, you may be forgetting that true superstars consistently commit to whatever they do.

It is possible to get your team to think, and act, like they own the business. You can get them to care just as deeply as you do. How do you do that? First, you'll need to be consciously aware of any assumptions you may have about performance management. Here are mine.

Five Key Assumptions about Leadership

Here are five key assumptions we will lean on about leadership and knowledge transfer. As you read them, take note of where you do—and do not—agree. My goal is not to convince you here. My goal is to give you a plumb line of sorts to bounce up against—so you can more consciously and clearly create your own tailored leadership mantra.

1. Knowledge alone is useless.
2. Situational success differs from systematic success.
3. Gaps in feedback exist.
4. A leadership mantra will minimize gaps.
5. A systematic success *formula* will enable your *mantra*.

Assumption #1: Knowledge Alone Is Useless

Have you ever heard the expression "Knowledge is power?" I completely disagree. "Knowledge" alone is *not* power. But when it is appropriately applied, or *systematically* transferred, knowledge becomes power.

Here's a weird question for you: Why are you so successful? What exactly does it take to be a success? You may immediately mention the traditional answers: work ethic, education, technical skills, focus, resilience, etc. Blah, blah, blah: Lots of unsuccessful people have those things. So, again, I ask: *Why* are you so successful?

Have you ever met a super-hard worker who failed to achieve his dreams? Have you ever been held hostage by the monologue of a technical wizard who couldn't answer basic questions in simple language? Possessing education, work ethic, and technical abilities does not guarantee the appropriate *application* of those skills necessary to achieve excellence. The most successful people systematically *apply* the knowledge they have in an appropriate way.

Assumption #2: Situational Success Differs From Systematic Success

SBOs are usually superstar technicians (or "doers") of their craft. Many quickly find, though, that they're much less capable at communicating or getting others to buy into their formulas for success. One key reason for this is that much of what they *systematically* "do" is invisible to them. Few SBOs are able to succinctly clarify how to be consistently successful. They just do it—time after time.

Distinguishing between situational and systematic success may help bridge the gap. *Situational* success is an in-the-moment, critical-thinking response to handle a specific challenge. *Systematic* success, comparatively, is a scalable process that you and others can use to consistently maximize potential for positive results. It's a series of actions that define "how" to best to consistently achieve results and enable the brand. Consider the situational versus systematic success comparison in Figure 4.1 on page 64.

A systematic success formula lays the core foundation for a more balanced leadership approach. It helps you to identify all your expectations and focus more on the pace and cadence of how your team is performing—much like an assembly line manager. A systematic approach can provide you with an "official" way to formally acknowledge, and measure, all those important soft skills most performance management programs ignore. More on that in Part III.

Figure 4.1—**Situational vs. Systematic Success**

SITUATIONAL SUCCESS	VS.	SYSTEMATIC SUCCESS
Dynamic, unique, and mostly random occurrence		Duplicative, scalable, disciplined process
Helps form trust in your systematic success formula		Serves as prep for situational success
More difficult to plan for		Easier to plan for
Less personal control		More personal control
Focuses on results		Focuses on process
Success now		Success over time
Wins "the battle"		Wins "the war"

Assumption #3: Gaps in Feedback Exist

Many SBOs struggle to separate systematic from situational feedback. How many times have you looked right past the situational successes of one of your team members because you were stuck on a bigger, systematic flaw in their process? If you think your answer is "never," I'd encourage you to think again. It may be occurring more than you realize.

A friend of mine—let's call her Anne—owns a consulting company. She shared with me her frustrations with her sales team's approach to securing new clients. During weekly staff meetings, when her sales team shared new (situational) sales they had made, Anne withheld her excitement. She considered the new sales "lucky" and not the result of a solid (systematic) sales approach. In other words, she was already thinking past the immediate situation.

See the gap? One person—in this case, the employee—is communicating from a situational perspective, while another—the SBO—is responding using a systematic lens. Gaps like this often demotivate a team by marginalizing the immediate win and the individual effort the win required. Worse still, the flaw in the systematic process—assuming there was one—still hasn't been resolved.

That means the SBO should expect the same conflict to recur in the very near future.

These types of microaggressions happen all the time and frustrate everyone involved. They are also extremely inefficient and very avoidable. The problem in this situation is that both the employee and the SBO are right–and they're both wrong. The solution is to close these gaps before they happen by creating a simple mantra.

Assumption #4: A Leadership Mantra Will Minimize Gaps

Chances are that very few folks on your team care as much about the business "vision statement" as you do. Part of the reason for this is because the business is *yours*; it's only natural for you to be completely invested in it. Vision statements are great, but rarely are they personal for anyone other than the SBO. Success, on the other hand, has everyone's attention. Most people want to be successful, even if only for their own selfish benefit.

Unlike many of your corporate counterparts who must function within a pre-existing hierarchy muddled with political nonsense and unwritten rules, you, as the SBO, have the unique opportunity to lead *your* way. Have you ever thought to yourself:

- They just aren't as motivated as I am.
- They're not as emotionally invested.
- They're not as smart.
- If only they would ______________ (fill in the blank) as intensely as I do.

Good news–you're not alone. Many SBOs feel some degree of resentment for anyone who doesn't seem as invested in the success of their business as they are. That's a pretty natural reason for tension. But your people *can be* as motivated, emotionally connected, and just as __________ (fill in the blank) as you are. The key to getting them there: Install a leadership mantra.

Think of your leadership mantra as:

The most important action-oriented word necessary for success. It's the thing each individual on your team, including yourself, can consistently do to maximize their chances for success, given the uniqueness of your business.

What's the one word, or mantra, that you have consistently leaned on over the years to be successful? In other words, what did you actually "do" in order to consistently achieve results?

The beauty of having a one-word mantra is that it's easy to install deeply into the minds of your team. It's a functional "thing" they can do. A clear mantra helps you align and connect each individual under your roof as a synergized team. You can lean on it in times of struggle, unlike that mystical vision statement which is collecting dust in your business plan.

A simple mantra may be easier for you to embrace by considering your industry or the customers you serve. Try answering these questions:

- What action, if consistently taken, will best protect our brand?
- What one mantra does our industry demand most?
- What key people skills, work ethics, and attributes are most necessary for success in my business?
- What's the one attitude, experience, or distinguishing factor about your business that you want placed deep in the minds of your customers?

Some potential industry-related examples are illustrated in Figure 4.2.

Figure 4.2—**Possible Industry-Related Mantras**

INDUSTRY	POSSIBLE MANTRA		INDUSTRY	POSSIBLE MANTRA
Marketing	Engage		Mediation	Negotiate
Medical	Heal		Legal	Resolve
Nonprofit	Serve		Self-Help	Inspire
Media	Report		Military	Adapt
Art	Create		Security	Protect

The examples offered in Figure 4.2 are not meant to be "right." It's OK to disagree with them, and, in fact, I challenge you to do just that. You decide what works best. You're the boss, and this is your mantra for your distinct business. Tailor away and trust your gut.

Pick a few themes that most resonate with you. Then bounce them off your team and trusted advisors. Don't worry about getting it "wrong," either. We'll talk about adjusting and tailoring mantras and formulas a little later. In fact, Chapter 11 is all about tweaking the system and actually rolling it out.

The important thing is that you deliberately choose a clear theme that you truly believe in and get it out of your head and into the minds of your team. Your most prized philosophies need to be externalized where your team can see, embrace, and ultimately duplicate them. Remember, knowledge alone is not power.

The benefit of a one-word mantra is that it's a simple handle your team can latch onto. The drawback is that there are too many different ways to interpret what that mantra means. Welcome to the case for the systematic success *formula*—that clarifies and enables your mantra.

Assumption #5: A Systematic Success Formula Will Enable Your Mantra

Now, this piece of the game may not be easy for everyone. Some of the SBOs that I've coached in the past have needed help developing the right mantra and formula for their business—and that's OK. This book is meant to ask the right questions to get you thinking about the key behaviors your business needs most. If you really just need an expert to come in and help you install a fully tailored performance management system, check out some of the options on my website (www.christophermcintyre.com).

That said, my intent is to guide you in creating a tailored formula on your own. Here's what a systematic success formula is:

Four or five actions required to achieve your mantra. If you expected everyone to actually make your mantra happen, what sequence of steps would they need to actually take?

The steps don't always have to be taken in order, but they do need to happen in varying degrees for your mantra to be consistently achieved. Book II in the Roadmap Series, *Motivating Without Money*, will show you exactly how to unpack the "Art" of your leadership approach—to determine where, and when, to focus on each step. But before you can expect it—your have to define it. Check out Figure 4.3 for a few examples of how you might turn a mantra into a measurable formula, then try breaking down a mantra of your own.

Figure 4.3—**How to Turn a Mantra into a Systematic Formula**

MANTRA	SYSTEMATIC SUCCESS FORMULA			
	STEP 1	STEP 2	STEP 3	STEP 4
ENGAGE	Define the Bulls-Eye	Stay Prepared	Create Opportunities	Take Action
SERVE	Listen	Assess	Empathize	Respond
INSPIRE	Connect	Probe	Educate	Direct
EXCELLENCE	Raw Desire	Attitude	Effort	Results

The big idea here is that you really can get others to be just as engaged in the success of the business as you are. It just takes a little extra focus around expecting technical skills and outputs, along with the right people skills, work ethics, and attributes for your business. It's about being as objective as you can about "how" to *systematically* do what you expect.

—Potential Systematic Success Formula: Engage

I'll use the rest of Part II to give you an example of how you might create a systematic success formula for the mantra: Engage! How do you remain *systematically* engaged? Better yet—how do you measure the systematic engagement of your team?

Systematic engagement happens by *defining* (D) what the bull's-eye (success) looks like given the uniqueness of the current circumstances. Once you have a clear sense of what success would look like, you can *prepare* (P) to achieve it. By staying prepared, you won't be afraid to proactively create *opportunities* (O) to *act* (A) on.

Systematic Engagement = (D) x (P) x (O) x (A)

- *Define* the Bull's-eye
- Stay *Prepared*
- Create *Opportunities*
- Take *Action*

Part III of this book will show you exactly how to install your core mantra. The next chapter takes a look at how to consistently define the new bull's-eye.

Figure 4.4—Chapter 4 Summary Checklist: Developing a Systematic Success Formula

OUTCOME	RATING
Strongly Agree	6
Agree	5
Somewhat Agree	4
Somewhat Disagree	3
Disagree	2
Strongly Disagree	1
KEY STATEMENTS	**RATING**
Checkpoint #1: Everyone here is crystal clear about our "secret sauce."	
a. I can clearly define what it is that's "special" about "how" we do what we do.	
b. I can define that feeling I want our customers to have when dealing with us.	
c. My team can define that feeling I want our customers to have when dealing with us.	
d. My hiring process is built to uncover superstars that are in line with our mantras.	
e. I've tied our secret sauce directly to our performance management system.	
Checkpoint #2: My team is clear on the distinct "mantra" that enables our brand.	
a. I realize knowledge alone is useless.	
b. I am clear on the key people skills, work ethics, and attributes (PEAs) that will best promote our brand.	
c. I stress and specifically expect key PEAs.	
d. I've worked with my team to discuss key PEAs that could bring us success.	
e. I can define a few good mantras most necessary for success in our industry.	
Checkpoint #3: I have a clear formula that clarifies "how" to systematically achieve our mantra.	
a. I distinguish between, and formally measure business metrics and key PEAs.	
b. I am clear about all the skills necessary for success given our brand.	
c. I communicate clearly by distinguishing between situational and systematic success.	
d. We have developed a systematic process that will check in with, promote, and protect our brand.	
e. I realize I can fully tailor the key PEAs to meet my business needs.	

Figure 4.4—Chapter 4 Summary Checklist: Developing a Systematic Success Formula, continued

Actions I could take to develop, and tailor, my own systematic success formula:
a.
b.
c.
d.
e.

Chapter 5

Systematic Engagement Step 1

Define the Bull's-Eye!

If you're going to be systematically engaged, it's critical to define—and redefine—the new bull's-eye. Regardless of whether you're in a meeting, or rolling out your annual strategy—the "bull's-eye" is the best thing you should be looking for, doing, or talking about. It's the main thing—and it's very elusive.

In business, priorities can be amorphous and dynamic. Defining success is all about your ability to stay sensitive to those changes and to help others shift their behaviors as necessary. This chapter offers tactical questions you can ask yourself and your team to keep focused squarely on the target. Let's start by defining success *now*.

Define Success *Now*

Have you ever begun your day with a carefully crafted plan for exactly what you need to accomplish, only to have the first phone call, email, or visitor completely change the game? How often do you feel like you can't get any of the "important" work done because of all the distractions? If you're like many SBOs, it happens more than you would like. Your priorities may shift multiple times throughout the day; for that reason, your definition of *success* should shift along with it.

Systematic success begins with defining what success looks like given the uniqueness of any given moment. This concept is simple but particularly difficult for busy SBOs to consistently maintain. Because success is a constantly moving target, your competitive advantage relies on your ability to recalibrate priorities and help your team find the bull's-eye at any given moment.

Consider staff meetings as a simple example. How productive are they for you? How about for your team? Team members often describe recurring staff meetings as productivity drains that take longer and are less productive than they should be.

Meeting mayhem can be created when the purpose of a meeting shifts constantly. The shift, though, isn't the problem. The problem is, the meeting leader often can't hold or shift the attention of the entire group at the same time. It's at precisely that point that group focus begins to leak.

- How well do I hold my group's attention during meetings?
- Are there any particular processes that tend to be facilitated too loosely?
- Who skews communication in the group? How do they do it and what can I do to stop it?

DO YOUR STAFF MEETINGS SUCK?

Think about it. Have you ever been in a meeting that turned to mush because half the group was talking about issue "A" while the other half of the group was stuck on issue "B"? Or maybe one person was trying to plan the action steps to an event while others in the group were still brainstorming potential problems? Where might your processes get muddled?

- When was the last time I led a conversation where I didn't hold the group's attention well? What happened? Where did it go off track?

I used the example of a meeting because it's easy to see the impact of not holding the focus *now* in that environment. In meetings, when the group is not focused, in sync, or discussing the most relevant issues, people mentally check out. Usually, when meetings go bad, the missing question should be: "What, exactly, are we trying to accomplish here, right now?" Try to keep that question consistently in the front of your mind.

Define Simple Short-Term Objectives

I used to subscribe to the idea that you couldn't guarantee success, but I've since canceled my subscription. Instead, I learned that I needed to define success more broadly, and to think about what it looks like in more situations. Even when I separated from the Air Force to become an inspirational speaker, I really had no clue what it meant to be a successful inspirational speaker, and I was pretty ignorant (and arrogant) about how to make it happen. It wasn't until I actually arrived in San Diego that I really started clarifying how I planned to become a professional speaker.

One of the most embarrassing moments I've ever had was due to my inability to define simple short-term objectives. When I first got to San Diego, I was ruthless about getting my name out there as a motivational speaker. When I finally got an interview with a local business leader, she asked me what I spoke about. I answered, "Um, motivation?" We shared an awkward 60 seconds staring at each other before she finally told me she'd "get back to me." I'm pretty sure she realized at that moment that I had no idea what I was talking about—and she was 100 percent right!

A new career is a pretty big thing to just jump right into, and chances are you rarely leap into big decisions as haphazardly as I did.

But how diligent, deliberate, and consistent are you about redefining success in even the small things like daily meetings, objectives, or guidance for your team members?

Here are a few spot-check questions that might help you consistently pinpoint specific and simple objectives for your group:

- Are we talking about systematic or situational success?
- What is a small success?
- What is a huge success?
- What should no longer be happening?
- What should start happening?
- What will be easier (or more difficult) to do?

By asking spot-check questions frequently, you can minimize a lot of miscommunication. You will also acquire a much better sense of your group's critical thinking skills. There will be times when you have to dig even deeper, but that doesn't mean you have to do all the defining. More on that soon.

Define What Success Is *Not*

If you find yourself struggling to clearly define successful objectives, try defining what success is *not*. You may stumble across a much cleaner definition of success by simply eliminating the options you *don't* want. With your particular project or situation, what does failure look like, and which actions lead to that result? This is a particularly useful strategy when brainstorming with your team.

Define What—and Ask How

Do you remember the *delegating* and *defining the soft stuff* conversation from Chapter 1? If not, let me refresh your memory. We discussed how *passion* could mean different things to different people, depending on their definition of passion. One simple way you can minimize communication gaps is to define what you expect–and listen for how it will occur.

Figure 5.1—**State "What" and Ask "How" Example**

STATE: WHAT I EXPECT	ASK: HOW CAN IT HAPPEN?
Tighten up customer service.	Decrease customer service complaints by 10 percent in the first quarter.
Be more of a team player.	Help Monica improve her MS Word skills so she can submit the audit report by February.
Improve communication skills.	Join Toastmasters—and check in with team on how I can improve my communication skills by end of month.

Notice how specific actions are assigned for each expectation. In this way, you can measure, by a certain time, whether your expectations were met.

- Did customer complaints drop by 10 percent in the first quarter?
- Did Monica learn to submit the weekly report by February?
- Did your team member join Toastmasters (a speaking organization), and what feedback did they get from others?

By defining what you expect–and asking your team members how they plan to accomplish those expectations–you can guarantee your goals are being clearly understood. Think about it. There are an infinite number of ways someone could "improve their communication skills," but not all of them are productive. By involving your team members in the decision-making process, you also maximize motivation, empowerment, accountability, and feelings of worth to the business.

This is not about micromanaging. This is about active listening and clearly defined expectations. It's about enhancing collaboration through being curious about how your team plans to achieve your expectations. Those examples in Figure 5.1 were easy; let's look at a few that aren't so simple in Figure 5.2 on page 78.

Stop reading, take two minutes, and answer the *how* questions in Figure 5.2. Most people can use some improvement in all of those areas,

Figure 5.2—State "What" and Ask "How"

STATE: WHAT I EXPECT	ASK: HOW CAN IT HAPPEN?
Improve your people skills.	
Develop a stronger work ethic.	
Improve teamwork.	

so try answering those questions for yourself first. Make sure you can actually measure your responses. Were your answers directly aligned with your business goals?

Then, give these questions to your team members in a staff meeting. See what kinds of answers they come up with. Are their answers specific? Do their answers align with your business goals? Finding specific answers to these vague questions will help everyone sharpen their communication skills.

In Part III of this book, I'll introduce a performance conversation form that will help you to clearly state "what"—and empower the "how." Your ability to empower your team to define *how* they will meet expectations is critical. Disconnects between *what* and *how* lead to organizational drag, blame games, lower morale, and increased people problems. One way to head off a blaming culture is to focus consistently on the things you can control.

—Define: Success You Can Control

The best way to lose your confidence is to consistently chase things that are completely beyond your control. Have you ever met someone who always complains about what others did? Or who always plays the victim by constantly moaning about external circumstances that can't be stopped?

Systematic engagement requires a focus on your options, not on your lack of options. What value is there in wasting already limited resources (time) complaining about things you can't control or change? By focusing on things that are out of your control, you multiply your chances of failure because there's always an *x* factor. But when you focus on the things you can control, you replace the *x* factor with a trusted multiplier: your effort.

Let's look at three examples of how you can consistently control your degree of success:

1. Align actions with objectives.
2. Protect vigor for the work.
3. Find success that excites you.

Align Actions with Objectives

Here's a spot check. If you had to repeat yesterday over and over again, would your actions have pointed you towards your objectives for the quarter? Sometimes we get so tied up with all the busy work that we don't even realize that the busy-ness shifts our focus from where it needs to be: our objectives. If you're always in fire-fighting mode, chances are your day is rarely spent productively working to meet your short-term objectives, let alone those longer-term goals.

As an SBO, you make hundreds of choices every day that are within your control. The sum of your choices determines your ultimate level of freedom. When those choices are primarily fueled by clear, short-term objectives, you can avoid unnecessary detours. More on how to create, and align, with clear objectives soon.

> **POP QUIZ**
> Look around your desk and at the emails in your inbox. Go through each one and ask yourself: Which of my goals does this email, letter, or piece of paper support?

Protect Vigor for Your Work

You will experience those exhausting days when you question why you ever went into business for yourself. As an SBO, you will stretch and, at times, overextend yourself. It happens. That is a given for anyone who's growing and pushing his or her limits.

But when I say, "protect vigor for your work," I am reminding you that you must protect yourself so that you consistently enjoy your craft. If that excitement, joy, and rookie energy are no longer present, you may need to schedule in more sporadic breaks, so you don't become another jaded business SBO who sees only the negative.

Jay Nelson, one of the SBOs I interviewed for this book, owns a heavy construction company in New England. His craft is seasonal. To keep himself excited about his work, he spends three months during the slow season sailing the southern U.S. shores every year on his boat. In fact, he was actually on his boat during our interview!

If you're reading this right now thinking, "Yeah, must be nice to be able to take three months off to sail every year—but I can't do that," remember to focus on what you *can* control. It's not about sailing a boat or taking three months off. It's about protecting a sustainable lifestyle that gives you the rest you need to protect your distinct ability to do excellent work. How are you doing with that?

Try answering these questions about protecting vigor.

- Are you still enthusiastic about the work you do?
- How are you protecting yourself mentally from burnout?
- Are you staying in decent physical shape?
- When you're "off," are you able to truly turn your mind "off" and not worry about job-related stuff?
- What's one (healthy) activity that usually tends to take your mind off of work? When was the last time you did it?

In business, it's common for work to ebb and flow. So you may currently be in a total state of reaction. You may not have any time for rest or relaxation given your business cycle. I understand that. The question here is more about your long-term patterns. In general, do you live in a total state of crisis that neglects and robs you of the time you need to recharge?

There is, and always will be, far more stuff to do than time to do it. You are the only one who can put boundaries in place that make protecting vigor for your work a priority. It may seem like you don't have time for rest, but if you're not getting enough of it, your ability to remain systematically engaged will suffer.

SBOs too often get trapped into becoming too busy to release their own pressure valves. Don't do that! Consider yourself no different than any other container with limited space and don't wait until you blow up to pay attention to your needs. While you're at it, expect your team to also do whatever they need to do to protect their vigor. If you do it, they'll do it. And when you do it and they do it, you will all have more mental energy to be excited about the needs of the business.

Find Success that Excites You

Follow the logic here. First, you're consistently defining what success *now* looks like. You're looking for success you can control, and you have far more options than you could possibly handle. How can you begin to see the tasks you need to act on as a great opportunity rather than an overwhelming chore? How can you shift your work from "yeah-yeah" (I'll do it) to "oh yeah!" (I look forward to doing it)? Check in with Figure 5.3.

Figure 5.3—**Define Work That Excites Me**

YEAH-YEAH . . .	OH YEAH!
Write a book.	Get my first book on the bestseller list.
Buy a house.	Buy a house so I can have dogs again.
Get a speaking credential.	Get speaking certification from National Speakers Association (since only 10 percent of speakers have it).
Get dental work handled.	Purchase an amazing smile that doesn't look like it was purchased.

One version (the "yeah-yeah") gets good things done in a chore-oriented way. The other (oh yeah!) version is genuinely exciting. Not only can I do all those things, but I'm attached to the benefit of making it happen. I know for some of you this may seem a little flowery, but lots of research demonstrates the power in visualization and positive thinking.

The point is you may want to make your most frequent tasks as psychologically attractive to look at as possible. That will take some of the sting out of having to actually achieve them. Use language that you genuinely believe in and trust; when you believe it, you'll be that much more motivated to prepare for it.

Speaking of preparing for success, what good is sitting around all the time and defining success? You've got to be prepared to act when opportunities come your way. Chapter 6 offers a tactical roadmap that shows you how to stay prepared.

Figure 5.4—Chapter 5 Summary Checklist: Define the Bull's-Eye

OUTCOME	RATING
Strongly Agree	6
Agree	5
Somewhat Agree	4
Somewhat Disagree	3
Disagree	2
Strongly Disagree	1
KEY STATEMENTS	**RATING**
Checkpoint #1: I consistently define success now.	
a. I'm quick to realize when my priorities have changed.	
b. I'm particularly sensitive to keeping my team focused in our meetings.	
c. I check in with my team on how well our meetings are run.	
d. I am good at keeping my team focused on the new bull's-eye.	
e. My team is good at consistently focusing on the new priorities on their own.	
Checkpoint #2: I consistently check for gaps in my communication.	
a. I frequently use spot-check questions to make sure we're aligned.	
b. I define "what" and empower the "how."	
c. I consistently listen for gaps.	
d. I develop my team to listen for gaps.	
e. I've recently asked my team where they've seen gaps.	
Checkpoint #3: I consistently look for success I can control.	
a. I don't waste time complaining about things out of my control.	
b. My team doesn't waste time focusing on what they can't control.	
c. I frequently check to make sure my actions are proactively aligned with my short-term objectives.	
d. I ruthlessly protect my vigor for my work.	
e. My to-do lists actually excite me.	

Figure 5.4—Chapter 5 Summary Checklist: Define the Bull's-Eye, continued

Actions I could take to more consistently define what success looks like:
a.
b.
c.
d.
e.

Chapter 6

Systematic Engagement Step 2:

Stay Prepared

We've established that in order to be consistently engaged we must first define what success looks like. Given the rapid pace of business today, success is dynamic in nature. So, the second phase of systematic engagement is about *preparation*. Will you be ready to act when the right opportunity arrives?

What if I were holding magic dust that could give you the opportunity of a lifetime? Let's say you were going to be interviewed on an international news channel to share information about your product or service with the world. That would be great, right?

But be warned: If you were to choose to take advantage of that opportunity, you would also need to be ready to field hundreds of calls and thousands of emails every week from around the globe, requesting your work. Would you be ready? Or would it be best for you—your team, your infrastructure, and your sanity—to put off the interview for another year until your business could handle the increased volume? That dilema happens to SBOs all the time.

This is an extreme example, and your situation probably doesn't have to be that grand. It could be a great new contract. Or

POP QUIZ
Are you consistently sharpening your skills so that you are always ready to take action?

it could come in the form of a call from a key competitor with an amazing partnership opportunity. If that kind of high-end opportunity presented itself on your doorstep, what knowledge, skills, and key PEAs would be made immediately visible for the world to see?

This chapter is about systematic preparation. Which of your current processes—if consistently adhered to—will mentally prepare you to handle the play of a lifetime?

Burn the Midnight Oil

On October 26, 1967, just six months before he was assassinated, Dr. Martin Luther King Jr. addressed a group of students at Barratt Junior High School in Philadelphia. He urged the students to "study hard and burn the midnight oil" so they would be ready when opportunities presented themselves in life.

Dr. Steven Jones, CEO of Jones & Associates Consulting, highlighted King's "burn the midnight oil" philosophy as one that stuck with him when he was creating his multimillion-dollar diversity and organizational change firm. He also cited his father's advice: "Most people are willing to work harder for someone else than they are for themselves." He put it this way when he described how he motivates himself to prepare for opportunities that have not shown up yet:

> *So when I'm up at night developing an assessment survey, or completing a final report, or analyzing a 360-degree feedback, or figuring out the right business plan (or whatever it is . . .)—I'm "burning that midnight oil"—and I'm thinking about Dr. King's speeches, and I'm thinking about my father, and I am willing to work harder for myself than I am for anyone else.*

Spend a few minutes answering the questions in Figure 6.1 on page 87 to see how well you burn the midnight oil.

Figure 6.1—Where Do I Burn the Midnight Oil?

SPOT CHECK: AM I CONSISTENTLY PREPARING MYSELF?	
In the past month, how have you burned the midnight oil?	
Did you catch yourself doing it (to inspire even more preparation in the future)?	
What is it you do, consistently, that motivates you to keep your skills sharp?	
What other ways have you motivated yourself to prepare for opportunities that haven't shown up yet?	

I've actually used this concept without realizing it. Not long ago I was returning home from delivering one of my public seminars in Boston. It was a late flight. Everyone around me was sleeping, but I had my light on, drafting the outline for this book, even though I was cramped in a coach seat. I typed a note to myself that said:

Everyone around me is sleeping, but I'm capturing thoughts for my first million-dollar book project. I'm winning the game right now.

Fast forward a year. I was on a flight coming back from coaching a small-business owner in London. It was very late at night, and everyone around me was, once again, deep in sleep as I was writing more of this book. This time, though, I was traveling in business class. I went back to the initial note I had written on that Boston flight and added:

. . . but now I'm in business class.

You may be thinking: "Hey, what if those other people were just sleeping before a big presentation" or "What if they were on vacation?" No, there's nothing wrong with getting rest, and definitely nothing wrong with a good vacation. Here's the thing, though: It's not about them. It's about me catching myself burning the midnight oil. It's about me motivating myself to continue doing it so that I have the confidence to act on the right opportunity at the right time.

So preparation is a good thing. But how can you find that mental balance between preparing and not being fearful about what you couldn't prepare for? How can you keep yourself from being overwhelmed? Actually, there's an easy way to do that.

Trust Your Inner Scrappy

Unlike your corporate counterparts, you may not be following in the footsteps of the CEO in front of you. Perhaps there was no general framework for "the way it used to happen," and you're making up a lot of the game as you go along. You need to have excellent critical thinking skills, yet you can't think too critically or it may impact your confidence level.

Trust your inner scrappy. Think less. Worry less. Trust your already proven ability to adjust in the moment. The less you think, the less your brain will freak you out.

Isn't it funny how some of the most brilliant people actually think themselves stupid? They'll overthink a plan, killing all the creativity and spontaneity that had made them successful in the first place. Overanalyzing also kills the genuine engagement of those around them and generates far more anxiety than most situations warrant. Mark Twain reportedly once said: "I'm an old man, and have known a great many troubles, but most of them never happened."

Taking in too much information can clog up your decision-making system with fear and conflicting ideas. I've seen countless SBOs research themselves into a panic. In particular, I've noticed two common ways SBOs think themselves stupid:

1. *The Terminal Patient:* freaks himself out every time he has a tiny problem. He'll search the web for the ailments and consistently convince himself the business is headed for an inevitable verdict: six weeks left to live.
2. *The Legitimist:* finds legitimate gaps in her current skill sets and worries too much on the front end about how she'll conquer the mountain that requires the use of that weak skill. She is always trying to solve problems that haven't shown up yet.

I'll bet your mind is sounding the alarm bells right now. You might be recalling all the situations where analysis and strategic planning have served you well. I agree that planning is a good thing. But there's definitely an opportunity cost of thinking too much and not trusting enough in your ability to adapt in the moment.

Here are some key "trust your inner scrappy" questions to ask yourself:

- At what point does planning become plaguing?
- How would you know you've hit that point?
- How many times have you mapped out a beautiful plan, only to have the entire game change after the first step?
- What areas do I plan a little too much in?
- In what ways do I overwhelm myself?

Think about how much you didn't know when you first went into business. You probably had no clue what you were really getting yourself into. If only you knew then what you know now, right? Chances are, you'll be saying the exact same thing ten years from now about what you didn't know *today*. You didn't know what you didn't know, and still you made it. Since history tends to repeat itself, chances are good you'll make it again. Why not plan on it?

The bottom line is that one often overlooked key to preparing for success is to actually prepare less. You won't be able to prepare for many of the situations coming your way in the future. Trust your inner scrappy to fight through challenge with a solution—and welcome mistakes along the way.

Lean into Your Mistakes

So you're burning the midnight oil, preparing for what hasn't shown up yet. And, since you couldn't possibly prepare for everything, you're trusting your inner scrappy to adapt on the fly. Let's face it, there will be bumps in the road. That's actually a good thing—when appropriately embraced.

Mistakes happen. When was the last time you caught yourself in one? Mistakes are usually so much easier to admit long after they've passed.

One SBO I know opened many general home-contracting businesses. He was very bright and an exceptionally hard worker. He earned his contractor's license after years of intense study. He really enjoyed working for himself and quit a cushy union contractor job making a six-figure salary to venture out on his own. He was a master at ripping apart kitchens, bathrooms, roofs, and any other part of a house or building. He was really good at quickly rebuilding *much* of what he tore down, too. Note that the operative word is *much*.

What happened next? His businesses were constantly being sued and always headed out of business. Why? He couldn't finish the jobs. He couldn't put sharp, clean edges on his work. Electrical outlet covers were crooked. The faucets leaked. The paint was blotchy. The roof shingles didn't align quite right. The driveways weren't perfectly level. Something was off every single time.

Some customers accepted the shoddy work, but most didn't. To his customers, the job simply wasn't complete. His finishing skills just weren't on par with his drive. Instead of using his high degree

POP QUIZ

Did you create one of those really cool, fully developed and way overanalyzed business plans before you started your business? If you did, how closely did you actually follow it as you've grown your business into the successful entity it is today? I'd be willing to bet that it caused more pain than gain during your growth. Mike Tyson, the famous boxer, once said, "Everyone has a plan . . . until they get punched in the face."

Figure 6.2—**Lean into Your Mistakes**

LEANING INTO MY MISTAKES	
What was a recent mistake I made?	
Why did the mistake happen?	
What level of effort did I put into correcting my mistake?	
How could I have responded to my mistake better?	
How did I handle my mistake well?	

of intellect and motivation to improve what he did poorly, he simply ignored his mistakes and–worse yet–made more of them faster.

Good luck with your business if you're playing that game. You need to have the courage to lean into the deficiencies that will keep you from finishing the race. You can't win the race if your shoes are always untied.

The simple questions in Figure 6.2 can help you assess yourself and how you handle your mistakes.

Answer these questions on your own, and then ask someone who was directly impacted by your mistake to answer them as well. This will help you find the gaps and give you a specific way to lean directly into your mistakes. It's particularly useful when you can bounce your self-assessments off a trusted mentor.

Find a +1 and +2 Level Mentor

Speaking of mentors: Do you have one?

Think about your financial growth for a minute. Remember how cool it was to earn that first dollar? Or being curious about how to hit the $200,000 mark for the first time? What about that $1 million mark? And once you hit $1 million, maybe the next obvious goal was $5 to 10 million, right? Then the $50 to $100 million mark? Perhaps you're now striving for the $100 + million—or thinking about going public.

Here are four simple mentor-oriented questions to consider.

1. Using the growth examples above, if you were to break down the financial tiers for your business what would they be?
2. What level are you currently at? ($200,000, $1 million, $5 to $10 million, etc.).
3. Do you have a mentor at the next (+1) level above you *outside* of your industry?
4. Do you have a mentor above the next level (+2) *inside* of your industry?

Caution! As SBOs get more and more successful (and consequently busier), they have a tendency to seek less and less assistance from mentors. Bad move. Even if you are completely content with your current revenue level, having a mentor at the next level could be helpful. Regardless of where you are now, there is another level. There's also someone *at* that next level—find him or her.

By consulting with the next (+1) level mentor outside of your industry, you could get good advice that's not bogged down by typical industry thinking errors. They may also offer fresh perspectives on industry challenges while bringing a more macro business case view to your issues. By finding a (+1) mentor outside of your industry, you won't have to worry about that mentor fearing you as competition. Of course, the disadvantage of a mentor outside of your industry is the flip side: She won't know the intricacies of your industry and may offer logic that only fits (or fits best) in her world.

Welcome to the case for (+2) mentors inside your industry. If they're at the +2 level, they know your game inside and out. These folks will be more likely to help add perspective to issues you will be likely to see while on your journey. Since they are at the (+2) level, they will probably be less likely to see you as immediate competition and more willing to genuinely share information. That said, you are still in the same industry, and (+2) mentors could be curious about acquiring you or sensitive about sharing niche secrets.

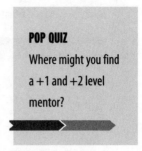

POP QUIZ
Where might you find a +1 and +2 level mentor?

By balancing your mentors within and outside of your industry, you win and further serve to prepare yourself for the big moment.

Figure 6.3—Chapter 6 Summary Checklist: Prepare for Success

OUTCOME	RATING
Strongly Agree	6
Agree	5
Somewhat Agree	4
Somewhat Disagree	3
Disagree	2
Strongly Disagree	1
KEY STATEMENTS	**RATING**
Checkpoint #1: I consistently prepare myself for the next "big thing."	
a. I actively catch myself burning the midnight oil.	
b. I could take that "next level" opportunity tomorrow, with confidence.	
c. I burned the midnight oil last month.	
d. I help my superstars catch themselves burning the midnight oil.	
e. I have created a culture that rewards consistent readiness.	
Checkpoint #2: I consistently trust my inner scrappy.	
a. I waste very little time worrying about my abilities.	
b. I know when my planning has become plaguing.	
c. I catch myself when I do too much thinking.	
d. I realize much of what's coming my way can't be prepared for.	
e. I know I will once again say, "If I knew then what I know now."	
Checkpoint #3: I lean confidently into my mistakes.	
a. I look forward to catching myself in the wrong.	
b. My superstars look forward to catching themselves making a mistake.	
c. My team feels comfortable helping me to see my mistakes.	
d. I have at least two +1 mentors outside of my industry.	
e. I have at least two +2 mentors inside of my industry.	

Figure 6.3—Chapter 6 Summary Checklist: Prepare for Success, continued

Actions I could take to be more consistently prepared to act on opportunities:
a.
b.
c.
d.
e.

Chapter 7

Systematic Engagement Step 3:

Create Opportunities

So we've seen that in order to be systematically engaged, you must first consistently define and redefine what success looks like. Then you find ways to stay prepared so that you won't fear fumbling the play of a lifetime. Now, with all that confidence under your belt, why not proactively create opportunities?

Create Opportunities That Force Action

Don't wait for opportunities to fall into your lap. That will happen—but not at the rate or time you'd prefer. Instead, create opportunities that will actually *force* you to act. Here are some ways you can *guarantee* exceptional opportunities for your business to act on.

Be of Use

T. S. Wiley, CEO of Wiley Protocol, suggests that one consistent way to find good opportunities is to simply be of use:

> *My father always said, "be of use"—and that meant to the whole world.*

Wiley was putting forth the notion that one should be curious about where the world looks for your attention. She also means that success can be found by serving the people and things most important to you. And, in that way, systematic success requires nothing more than your time and strategic focus.

Finding a place where you can be of use is one of the quickest and easiest ways to consistently create opportunities that will force you to act. Wiley was simply trying to be *of use* for a few friends when she applied her medical experience to ease their pains stemming from menopause. She matched her unique skill set with the needs of women around her and created a topical hormonal cream that could help relax some of their symptoms.

Wiley was being *of use* when her good friend (later turned business management wizard) Caren Abdela urged her to periodically present her game-changing concepts to a group of menopausal women in the neighborhood. She didn't know it at the time, but by simply being *of use*, her small neighborhood chat—along with Caren's ruthless tactical leadership—would ultimately propel her business into the national spotlight. She's now widely recognized as a leading voice in this area and was called on by the Senate to offer her expert perspective.

You don't need to be a highly specialized scientist or have the skills to manufacture some high-tech gizmo. Look around to see where you can be *of use* to someone. Maybe that person is an intern who stinks at building budget spreadsheets. Or perhaps it's your oldest employee who needs a boost of confidence because she's starting to feel irrelevant and threatened.

POP QUIZ

How much of your time is wasted "not" being of use?

On the flip side, how much time do you spend involved in conversations where you can't contribute in a meaningful way? Ask yourself the following questions during all your interactions: Am I being *of use* here? How could I possibly be *of use*? The next time you're stuck in an unproductive conversation, ask, "How can I be *of use* for you right now?"

That could help move the conversation away from idle chatter and closer to meaningful actions.

Leverage the Weiji

The Chinese word for "crisis" is *Weiji* (shown in Figure 7.1), which literally translated means: in danger (*wei*) is opportunity (*ji*). I couldn't agree more. Wild fluctuation is a part of business, and your ability to be *of use* in dangerous times is critical for your systematic success—and overall long-term freedom.

Did you know that Bill Gates started Microsoft during a recession? Now, you may not be interested in Microsoft or anything nearly as big. You probably are, however, interested in finding ways to survive the unavoidable downtimes. James Carter, CEO of Be Legendary, shared a brilliant example of this principle at work in his business.

On September 1, 2001, just ten months after going into business, Be Legendary secured a $250,000 team-building contract with the government. Ten days later, the 9/11 terrorist attacks occurred. Needless to say, the contract fell through. In that instant, Be Legendary was financially devastated.

Figure 7.1—**Embrace the Weiji**

James and his then-partner tried scraping together all the team-building activities they had to sell so companies could build morale on their own. Unfortunately, businesses didn't have the discretionary funding necessary to purchase even the cheapest activities.

James realized their traditional business model—selling products leading to bigger-ticket, in-house consulting assignments—wasn't working, so he decided to give the team-building activities away for free on his website.

James's business partner tilted like a pinball machine. Giving product away was clearly a deviation from the traditional consulting code. This created tension between James and his partner, but James saw the need and the opportunity to leverage the *Weiji.*

Then a funny thing happened. The phone actually began to ring again. SBOs and training managers from many of the *Fortune 100* companies started calling. They were looking for phone coaching on how to utilize the activities they had downloaded from the website. There was just one small problem. They couldn't afford the phone coaching or in-house presentations. This was a dangerous (*Wei*) unintended consequence of giving away the training. A large amount of James's time was being spent offering free phone coaching to the community.

But James saw the opportunity (*ji*) and continued to offer free phone consultations to anyone genuinely in need. Again, James's partner struggled to see the opportunity because he was choosing to focus on the danger. But James realized—and ultimately leveraged—an inside line to training managers and was able to observe the unique challenges their organizations were facing.

Traditional team-building companies who didn't have James's vision weren't talking to their clients and were therefore disconnected from the current internal business climate. James saw that. Consequently, he was able to understand the new environment that most training reps

Download James's interview to hear about how you can install more trust into your business culture.

were dealing with, and so he created a new line of curriculum directly addressing the new realities of the industry.

Soon enough, a major Fortune 100 company was conducting an executive meeting addressing morale issues. One of the training managers to whom James had previously offered free consulting presented the "Building a Dream" program as an option to the board. The executive in charge of the meeting declared, "That's it—that is exactly what we need now." They paused the meeting to call James right then and there.

James picked up a $1.2 million contract that day. Had he not been flexible enough to realize that the traditional consulting model was no longer applicable, he would have gone out of business. Take off the blinders of fear and find the *Weiji*.

Burn the Right Bridges

Another great way to *create opportunities* to act is to burn "the right" bridges. I am not referring to burning bridges by deceiving those who trust you, making enemies, or any other types of negative action. Burning your bridges in this context is meant to encourage forward-thinking actions that will eliminate (burn) old options that may have previously served you. Gandhi once said, "Jump—and the net will appear."

Phil Thearle, owner of Philip Thearle's Autowerks, a Collision Center (www.ptautowerks.com), purchased, moved into, and completely renovated a multimillion dollar, 75,000-square-foot, state-of-the-art collision restoration center. Phil's collision center—boasting many best-in-class technologies for his field—developed a revolutionary traffic flow pattern where vehicles could literally be systematically wheeled through consecutive work stations. This approach completely eliminated internal congestion and kept his workers from stumbling over each other to get their work done.

But there was one small issue with Phil's groundbreaking new building. At the time he purchased it, he didn't have enough savings,

POP QUIZ

- What's one great business opportunity you've been procrastinating on pursuing?
- What's one bridge you can burn, that could force you to move forward on it?

nor was he generating the revenue to cover its expenses. He burned a bridge with his old building because he opted out of the lease. The building was on the verge of being sold to another anxious SBO.

Phil forced forward movement. He trusted his intuitive vision about moving into the new building, creating the kind of revenue he needed to cover expenses. Ten years later, he's being interviewed for this book. He had the guts to jump and trusted the leap would create opportunities to act on more business. Good thing he did too. Collision experts from all across the country travel to Phil's center for facility tours.

Consider Figure 7.2 as a way to help you make a more informed "gut" choice on a daily basis.

There's a difference between burning bridges and doing something insane. I know better than to offer a "rule" here on how to know when (and when not) to burn bridges, because your inner skeptic would instantly find the exception. There is one consistent message, though,

Figure 7.2—**The Bridge-Burning Questionnaire**

BEFORE BURNING A BRIDGE—ASK:	
What's the worst that could happen?	And if it does, what will I do?
On a pain scale of 1 (minor annoyance) to 10 (I'd die)—what # would I give the worst?	In what instances will I accept a 1? In what instances will I accept a 10?
What's the best thing that could happen?	And if it does, what could I do?
On a pleasure scale of 1 (cool) to 10 (game changer for my business)—what # would I give the best?	In what instances will I accept a 1? In what instances will I accept a 10?
At what point in time will I have waited too long to act?	What opportunities may I have missed?
Is my "gut feel" telling me to do this?	Why?

that I've heard many SBOs echo when considering risk: Trust your gut—and blame no one else for your results.

No More Blaming "Them, That, or It"

You can condition yourself to see more opportunities by focusing less on "them, that, or it." In other words, focus primarily on the things *you* can control—and avoid the seductive temptation to victimize yourself by blaming others for subpar results. While delivering personal productivity seminars around the globe, one of the most interesting (and frustrating) things I noticed was how people were consistently committed to complaining about circumstances beyond their control.

When I asked directly "What gets in your way of being productive," they would primarily cite things like: co-workers (them), emails (that), phone calls (that), meetings (it), the boss (them), slow computers (it), etc. Even when I framed the question in terms of "What do *you* do that gets in *your* way of being productive," they would still struggle to avoid naming external factors that were completely beyond their control.

To be fair, many times the complaints were completely on target, which is why they were so emotionally charged. The boss *was* erratic and inefficient. The staff *did* attend lots of poorly run meetings. Their computers *were* slow. But after we got all that external stuff out on the table, I'd say, "OK, since those things are completely out of your control, how much time, mental energy, and sleep have you been losing over things you can't change?" How is holding on to that kind of stuff serving you?

For argument's sake, let's just assume that 20 percent of your day is wasted dealing with "them, that, or it" nonvalue-added issues. If you spend another 20 percent of your day *complaining* about that fact, 40 percent of your day is gone. That's like starting a daily productivity test with a "D." Add the numbers up over the course of a year, and you can see the cost of consistently blaming them, that, or it.

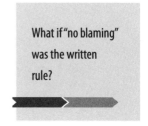

> **What if "no blaming" was the written rule?**

There is a more positive option. What if you *increased* your productivity by a measly 10 percent, simply by focusing more on the "you-oriented" issues necessary for improvement? In other words, what if you were consistently curious about the things you can do to be of better use—*now*? And let's just say that by doing that, you also inspired your superstars to do the same thing. If you had 15 employees, each increasing their productivity by 10 percent, you'd have a great year, more sleep, and more freedom!

We're all human. And we all really enjoy a good "it's all their fault, there's nothing more I could do" cry. Have at it. It's impossible to never waste time, get frustrated, or vent about things (both in and out of your control).

But the bigger point here is to be sensitive to where the numbers might be negatively skewed for you. What tiny gains in productivity can you consistently expect by a small shift in focus? That small shift in focus may be all you need to see a great opportunity right underneath your nose.

Of course, all the opportunities in the world are useless—if not *acted* on. Welcome to the last element consistently required for systematic engagement: Take Action.

Figure 7.3—Chapter 7 Summary Checklist: Create Opportunities

OUTCOME	RATING
Strongly Agree	6
Agree	5
Somewhat Agree	4
Somewhat Disagree	3
Disagree	2
Strongly Disagree	1
KEY STATEMENTS	**RATING**
Checkpoint #1: I consistently find opportunities to be of use.	
a. I found two significant ways to be of use last month.	
b. I catch my superstars, in the moment, being of use.	
c. I am quick to remove myself from situations when I'm being of minimal use.	
d. I can identify one opportunity I missed last quarter to be of use.	
e. I check with my superstars to see where they need me to be of more use.	
Checkpoint #2: I leverage the Weiji (find opportunity in danger).	
a. I actively try to find opportunities in dangerous situations.	
b. I develop my team well to leverage the Weiji.	
c. I lean on this concept while in wild fluctuation.	
d. I can name at least two examples of how I leveraged the Weiji last quarter.	
e. I can cite an example of where I should have (but didn't) leverage the Weiji last quarter.	
Checkpoint #3: I burn bridges to force positive forward movement.	
a. I know when to burn a bridge.	
b. I can confidently burn even a bridge that's good for me.	
c. I can cite an example of a positive bridge I burned this year.	
d. I have actually calculated the cost of blaming others and making excuses.	
e. I actively coach my team not to blame or make excuses for results.	

Figure 7.3—**Chapter 7 Summary Checklist: Create Opportunities,** continued

Actions I could take that could create more opportunities to act on:
a.
b.
c.
d.
e.

Chapter 8

Systematic Engagement:

Take Action

Teaching your team to be systematically engaged is possible. First, you frequently *define* the moving target of success. Second, you *prepare* and burn the midnight oil, certain that great opportunities will appear. Third, you can be certain opportunities will appear because you actually *create opportunities* that force forward movement. If you think about it, all of the previous principles lead to a proactive step four: *action*!

Make Taking Action Easier

This final chapter in Part II is meant to help make consistent *engagement* (the mantra I chose to work through) easier to actually do. Before we plug the systematic success formula for this mantra directly into a performance management system in Part III, let's look at simple ways you can motivate yourself—and your team—to take action.

What Is "Just" the "Next" Action?

David Allen, CEO of the David Allen Company and author of *Getting Things Done* (Penguin, 2001), discusses the timeless subtleties of the "next-action" concept in his book. What the *next-action* concept asks is when it comes to moving a particular project forward, what is literally the *very next* physical, visible action you need to take? While the concept seems simple enough, I can't tell you how many very bright people struggle to make the simple choice: What is first?

Assuming there's no psychological disconnect at play, one of the fundamental reasons many SBOs struggle with this question is primarily *because* they are so bright. They see so many potential consequences of taking action that they cripple their ability to make simple decisions.

There's a very slippery nature to the next-action concept. Our minds tend not to gravitate to the *true* "first" action. We skip the actions we might consider irrelevant or minimal, causing us to trip over our own shoelaces without ever realizing it. In other words, many people begin thinking about the consequences of step two, or three, or . . . you get the point.

As an example, let's say you're interested in doing something really exciting, like going to the dentist. The next step, you might think, is to just call and make the appointment. Simple enough, right? Simple, yes. Easy, no. Calling the dentist may not really be the very next action. First, do you even have the number? I realize this may seem like a petty distinction, but play along with me for a minute.

Let's say you once had the number, but you lost it somewhere at home. When you look at your to-do list, if it says "call the dentist," there is a high likelihood that you'll consistently procrastinate. That's not just because you may not like the idea of going to the dentist, but also because you don't have the number, and while your subconscious realizes that, your conscious may not. Calling the dentist won't happen as efficiently as it could have.

Figure 8.1—What's "Just" the Next Step?

END RESULT	TINY FIRST STEP
Quarterly objective: Establish two new corporate clients this quarter	**Next Action**: Look online to purchase cold-call lists **Not the Next Action**: Make cold calls
Quarterly objective: Develop our team's "mantra"	**Next Action**: draft a list of questions for our clients **Not the Next Action**: Interview clients to see what they say our mantra should be

I use the above example just to make the point, but trust me when I tell you: This concept can be life changing. I've personally witnessed the next-action concept transform the lives of hundreds of busy, productive professionals, just like you.

Now, sometimes your best next action is to lower the bar on some of your expectations for yourself–and even for your team.

Lower the Bar

You can systematically inspire your team to take more action by simply lowering the bar. This idea may seem almost incomprehensible to you, but it's often one of the best options consistently overlooked by many hard-charging SBOs. Think about a stringed instrument, such as a guitar, as an example. The musician (SBO) must make sure that the tension in the string (or employee) is perfectly tuned in order to make a premium sound (optimal output).

When the guitarist puts too much tension on the string, at best, it pings notes that are too high (creating negative stress) and, at worst, snaps altogether (loses all control). When the instrument doesn't have enough tension on the string, it sluggishly belches off-key notes, or worse, it may be of no use at all. This is one of the primary ways nightmares are created. Try answering the questions in Figure 8.2 on page 110.

Figure 8.2—**Lowering the Bar**

LOWERING THE BAR	
Where can I lower the bar for myself this quarter?	
Where can I lower the bar for a business goal?	
Do I have any employees chasing objectives that are a bit too out of reach? How can I lower the bar?	

It's simple to see the value of decreasing the tension in a stringed instrument, but how well do you apply this concept to yourself or your team? How quickly are you able to realize you have tuned the string (your team) too tightly? How quickly do you realize you have tuned your own strings too tightly? What does the optimal tune of your business sound like? Because you don't have the world of music to tell you how D-minor or E-flat guitar notes should sound, what music sheet are you using to calibrate the emotional melody of your team?

Let's go back to 9/11 one last time. At that time, businesses were forced to adjust their business success philosophy from "thrive" to "survive." Unfortunately, many of those businesses made that adjustment too late and went under. When danger looms, SBOs require the sensitivity to know when to simply lower (or shift) the bar for success.

James Carter, CEO of Be Legendary, example of realizing the game had changed for his team-building company is a perfect example. He lowered the bar from *thrive* to *survive*. By focusing on the things that were in his control, and by looking for opportunities to be of use, he was able to see things his partner—who remained in *thriving* mode—couldn't.

While I don't know the exact nature of your business model, I do know you've experienced varying levels of motivation from your employees. Getting premium sound from your team means being able to tighten and loosen the right strings at the right time. How will you know when it's time to lower the bar?

Don't forget that even the finest musicians miss notes. Luckily for you, most of the time, lots of people witness when you screw up. Admit it. Own it. *Publish it.*

Publish Lessons from Your Failures

If you're consistently challenging yourself–and most SBOs strive to do that–you will at some point fail. Failure's not a bad thing. But not making the most of a failure is a bad thing. Why not expect the entire team to be OK with identifying and learning from everyone's mistakes?

Not long after I moved to San Diego, I saw an ad from Monster.com's "Making It Count" speaking program. Basically, Monster contracted professional speakers to deliver motivational programs to high schools and colleges across the country. Bingo! This was my big chance. I posted my resume, tailored my strategic cover letter and knew they'd call me back offering an opportunity–which they did.

Soon, I got the Making It Count scripts in the mail to be memorized and presented at a national certification. I practiced the scripts with all the passion I could muster. I typed out the scripts. I recorded myself delivering the scripts on audio and video. I have no idea how many hours I spent burning the midnight oil for that presentation. I knew I'd be ready when I finally took the stage.

When certification time came, not only did I pass, but I also won top honors out of hundreds of speakers nationally. It was one of the most awesome and emotionally overwhelming experiences I've ever had. In that moment, I realized I'd burned the right bridge by separating from the military.

I did so well at the certification that Monster actually invited me–along with a handful of their top veteran speakers–to deliver one of their brand-new pilot programs. It was really an honor because no other rookies were invited. In my mind, I'd "arrived," and there was no turning back. I had an exceptional first semester delivering the seminars and was pegged as one of Monster's best speakers nationally.

Fast forward to the second semester. Because of my newfound confidence, I didn't practice nearly as hard. I figured I'd just wing it and wow everyone again. I figured very wrong.

This time around, there was a buzz as I took the stage because everyone expected me to be a superstar. I completely bombed. Right there in front of hundreds of professional speakers, I demonstrated a significant lack of preparation. They told me to go home, and I wasn't certified. It was one of the most humiliating experiences in my life and one I'll never forget.

At that point in my career, I was really starting to establish myself as a national speaker. I was being interviewed on radio stations and profiled in national magazines and books. I was no longer in a financial pinch. I didn't need the Monster contract and had all the motivation in the world to just forget that embarrassing situation and move on. Instead, I chose to lean into it and *publish the lessons from my failure.*

First, I called the folks at Monster and apologized for wasting their time. Next, I memorized my scripts and earned my second certification properly. Once that was accomplished, I asked for an opportunity to publish my "failure" experience in their monthly newsletter. I knew the article would help motivate future speakers struggling to burn the midnight oil for their presentations. The article also forced me to analyze my poor choices and gave me an opportunity to make the bad good.

Now let's bring this concept back to your world. Everyone makes mistakes every day, and SBOs are no exception. Yet too many SBOs miss the opportunity to lean into their failures while they are occurring. If you were to do so, not only would you learn from the mistake, your team would see firsthand that you are human. What if once a quarter

QUARTERLY BLUNDER LEARNING BLOG

- What functional position was it?
- What was the person's intent?
- What was the blunder?
- What was the impact?
- What could be done to keep the blunder from happening again?
- Any other key learning that might be useful for a future blunderer?

you, and everyone on your team, posted at least one noteworthy misstep into a blunder blog—and discussed it?

If you're like most SBOs, many of your best—and most difficult—lessons are still planted solely in your head, where no one can see or benefit from them. Knowledge alone is useless. The more your team sees you lean into your mistakes, the more readily they'll admit their own. Remember, just because you failed at a particular task doesn't make you a failure. It simply means a certain set of actions did not achieve the desired outcome.

Make Being OK with OK—*Not OK*

Before we look at how to install your success formula into your performance management system, let's look at one last aspect of consistent action. While interviewing the SBOs for this book, I noticed that all of them had committed themselves to a higher level of work than most people. They all shared a common thread of simply not being "OK" with just "OK work." Their standards of performance are just higher than those most people normally set for themselves.

Dr. Steven Jones (Jones & Associates) said it this way:

Many people do not hold themselves to a high standard of excellence and performance. I learned a long time ago that even though you're a small company you should think like a big company. When people see your materials they should think that they're dealing with IBM. Your company image, professionalism, and the way you talk to people—whether you're in a suit (as a man or a woman) and you're sitting down in an office with a beautiful view on the 29th floor, or you're at home with a robe on growing your company—always keep a high level of excellence . . .

David Stebbins (The Stebbins Group) addressed it similarly:

One of the things about being successful, and anyone reading this will think I'm arrogant and I am arrogant. There is a reason why only certain people get rich. One of them is that I insist on performance that's much higher than the average person is either able or willing to give.

It's important to distinguish between *effort* (trying) and *excellence* (high-level impact). Steven and David are both referring to excellence in a way that suggests holding yourself to higher standards. Yes, they put in extra effort, but they also ensure their efforts lead to high-value outcomes. Effort isn't enough.

Many highly capable people seem unwilling to choose that kind of high-level commitment. Some people dwell on their solid effort. Others may offer strong but extremely inconsistent impact. Both consistent effort and excellence are necessary for long-term systematic success and your freedom.

Just for fun, generate a list of your employees including yourself. Next, think of a key project recently completed by each person in the not-too-distant past. Now, based on a scale of one (little) to five (lots), go through that list distinguishing between, and rating, the overall effort and excellence each individual put into that particular project. Figure 8.3 on page 115 provides an example of how to evaluate both effort and excellent results.

Figure 8.3—**The Effort vs. Excellence Distinction**

NAME	PROJECT: CANADA	EFFORT	EXCELLENCE
Me	Revamp New Strategic Plan	5	5
Ben	Revamp New Strategic Plan	2	2
Joe	Revamp New Strategic Plan	2	4
Kia	Office IT Rollout	4	3
Mary	Office IT Rollout	5	4
Mike	Office IT Rollout	1	2

Take a look at the above table and consider how you might best use these numbers. Just separating your feedback about *effort* from your feedback about *excellence* might be valuable enough for you. Perhaps you've never distinguished between the two when communicating with your team. This is particularly useful when giving specific performance feedback to your superstars. You may also use a table like this when pairing up teams. You could pair your high-effort folks with high-excellence folks on certain projects.

When debriefing new initiatives or product rollouts, you may ask more questions of your high-effort folks concerning what they did during the process. You could lean more on your excellence folks to discuss the impact of the products on your customers. Try tracking a few random projects in this way throughout the year. It could reveal to you trends and themes for certain individuals you wouldn't have normally realized.

You may also find that certain people tend to rationalize that their lack of one skill is compensated by strong production in another. For instance, Joe may lean more on his natural skills and abilities to produce excellent (4) work as justification for giving minimal (2) effort. He may even disregard opportunities to place more effort into his work simply because he's already producing better work than most of the team.

Make being OK with OK–*not OK*! Even for high performers like Joe. If other team members see you accepting Joe's (2) effort, regardless of his excellence, then you should be OK with accepting their (2) effort. We'll spend a lot more time on this concept in Book 2 of the Roadmap Series when discussing motivating without money. But for now, just remember: The expectation for everyone should always be to be better.

Now it's time to connect your core team to your core systematic success message. Part III, *Install Your Core Mantra*, will show you exactly how to do it–step by step.

Figure 8.4—**Chapter 8 Summary Checklist: Take Action**

OUTCOME	RATING
Strongly Agree	6
Agree	5
Somewhat Agree	4
Somewhat Disagree	3
Disagree	2
Strongly Disagree	1
KEY STATEMENTS	**RATING**
Checkpoint #1: I consistently ask "What's the next action?"	
a. I make highly efficient choices.	
b. I minimize overanalysis.	
c. I rarely overwhelm myself by considering too many options.	
d. I help my team simplify complex issues by using the next-action concept.	
e. I minimize procrastination by using the next-action concept.	
Checkpoint #2: I know when to lower the bar.	
a. I understand the value of lowering the bar sometimes.	
b. I can cite an example of how I lowered the bar within the last quarter.	
c. I have an example of when I didn't lower the bar this year—but I should have.	
d. I have an example of lowering the bar this year when I shouldn't have.	
e. I know what melody my team makes emotionally—when they're optimally tuned.	
Checkpoint #3: Consistently being OK is not OK for anyone on my team.	
a. Systematically speaking, I consistently expect excellent results.	
b. I distinguish between effort and excellence.	
c. I consider the effort and the excellence, distinctly, for all team members.	
d. I reward both effort and excellence.	
e. I have the courage to publish my failures.	

Figure 8.4—**Chapter 8 Summary Checklist: Take Action,** continued

Here are some ways I could make taking consistent action easier on myself (or my team):
a.
b.
c.
d.
e.

Part III

Install Your Core Mantra

Craft the right team. Create a consistent core message. Now, simply connect the two. Remember in Part I, I promised we'd discuss exactly how to handle the time in between your employees' first day and that 90-day check-in period? That's precisely where your performance management program comes in. This final section is all about having and documenting timely, focused, and consistent performance conversations.

A rock-solid performance management program helps you:

- Clarify *all* of your most valuable assets and consider how to consistently nourish them.
- Align your superstars using your systematic success formula.
- Empower your superstars by enabling candid multidirectional conversations about the right performance drivers.

From scheduling when to have your performance conversations to staying on topic in those conversations to executing your program, I think you will find this section of the book to be a very thorough checklist to guide your implementation step by step. First, though, let's look at how to install the framework for consistently focused performance conversations.

Chapter 9

The Quarterly Conversation

I'm sure you're familiar with those traditional annual performance management (PM) models. Think back to a job you had where you weren't the boss. Remember that document the boss would pull out once a year and blow the dust off of? It was full of wish-list-type goals that neither of you really paid much attention to throughout the year. You might have even ghostwritten your own appraisal once or twice, right?

Remember how those PM conversations went? They were pretty much useless and usually focused only on the past few months, ignoring two-thirds of your performance for the year. Worse yet, the boss never asked for your feedback and rarely took action if you gave it anyway. If you experienced anything similar to that process, what you may have learned was simple: PM is pretty much a waste of time.

If you've ever had that thought, I would agree with you—halfway. Those types of traditional PM programs usually are a big waste of time. At this point in the book, though, you should realize that a well-done PM absolutely must happen. Superstars, like all things that grow, must be nurtured, developed, and calibrated to function optimally.

In other words, the problem is not performance management, *per se,* but the process being used. There are actually two distinct problems with the traditional process. The first problem is the frequency of the performance conversation itself. Given the dynamic pace of business today, a year is just too long to wait for that crucial conversation. The second problem is a poorly delivered and horribly managed program.

Let's address the timing piece of the equation first and then untangle the program issues. Quarterly PM programs trump annual programs because they:

- Require SBOs to have longer-range goals to guide superstar objectives.
- Minimize surprises.
- Give employees frequent chances to correct their behavior.
- Give SBOs more opportunities to reinforce what is (and is not) working.
- Help keep the context for behaviors and choices fresh.
- Empower multidirectional collaboration instead of top-down dictation.
- Provide focused documentation needed when it's necessary to eject nightmares.
- Fit neatly with a 90-day, new-hire probationary approach.
- Force SBOs to take a proactive versus reactive leadership style.

Given all these benefits of the quarterly conversation, I challenge you to make a good case for the annual approach. In business, a year is a really long time. Priorities change. Markets shift. People come. People go. A quarterly approach helps—and actually requires—you to adjust your focus to what's most important.

Before we get into it, I realize your inner skeptic may be ringing the "Yeah, but I don't have time to do this" alarm. Squelch that voice. As a reminder, we'll directly address how to find the time in Chapter 11. For now though, really try to focus on the mechanics of this approach and how you can tailor it to work best for you.

The 90-Day Performance Conversation Model

Figure 9.1 gives you a quarterly PM template that you can adjust as necessary. Consider this entire approach, along with its measures, as a loose guideline for you to discuss, develop, and tweak with your team. Let's assume that we're talking about the first quarter of a year: January, February, and March.

Figure 9.1—**The 90-Day Model**

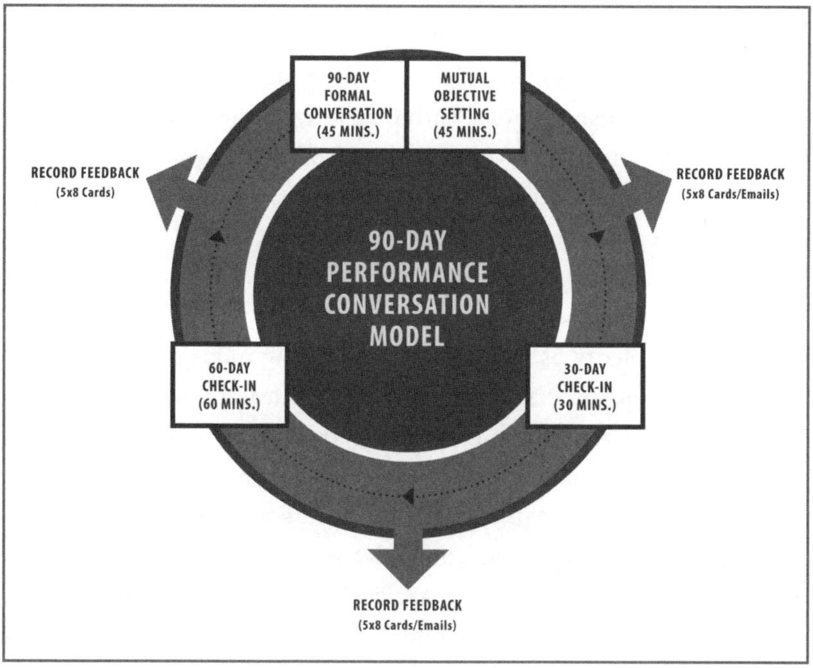

Step 1: Mutual Objective Setting

The primary purpose of the *mutual objective-setting* conversation is to establish quarterly objectives for your superstars. Consider this step truly "mutual." If you don't, you're probably doing too much of the thinking. Remember, you already went through all the hard work of crafting a dream team. You didn't do all that work just so you could always be the smartest person in the room, did you?

By sharing this conversation, you're telling the team they're smart too and that you expect them to prove it. In this way, you empower your superstars to contribute to the business in a meaningful way. They will fully support what they feel like they've helped to create. There are four simple things you can do to focus, share ownership, and improve the quality of your mutual objective-setting conversations.

Objective-Setting Success Factor #1: Distinguish Between Goals and Objectives

One key to owning a world-class PM program lies in your ability to clearly link key business goals with quarterly employee objectives. One way to ensure that happens is to distinguish between *goals* and *objectives.* While there are many, let's borrow a *goal* definition from David Allen; he defines a goal as a one- to two-year desired outcome.

Figure 9.2 on page 125 shows the difference between annual goals and quarterly objectives.

There are plenty of really good goal-setting models out there, so I won't waste time discussing them here. The idea of breaking big goals down into smaller, more achievable objectives is the important concept that we'll lean on moving forward. It's critical that you have very clear, relevant, and specific goals for your superstars to shoot for.

I'd highly encourage you to involve your superstars in your larger goal-setting process too. Doing so will help fully anchor them to the context behind your business strategies, which will help them be better prepared to make tough decisions when you're not around. Involving your superstars in the goal-setting process also offers them added

Figure 9.2—*Annual* Business Goals vs. *Quarterly* Superstar Objectives

BUSINESS GOALS (1- TO 2-YEAR OUTCOMES)	SUPERSTAR OBJECTIVES (QUARTERLY OUTCOMES)
Grow the business to $20 million	Establish two new corporate clients
Get book on *The New York Times* bestseller list	Finish research for Chapter 8
Install new PM program in our business	Develop our team's "success formula"
Determine return on investment for last year's sales trainings	Compare last year's training costs with student course evaluations

motivation when creating their own quarterly objectives, since they helped create the goal.

Objective-Setting Success Factor #2: Expect Team Members to Create Their Own Quarterly Objectives

A second great way to maximize the initial objective-setting conversation is to expect your superstars to determine how they'll pursue your longer-range goals this quarter. Remember that concept from Chapter 4? You clarify *what* goals you want achieved and guide each superstar to lead the conversation around to *how* they'll contribute to achieving them.

Here are three primary benefits of expecting superstars to create their own objectives:

1. It forces you to have clear goals. If your goals need a little clarifying, then you will hear about it through the objective-setting conversation.
2. It helps you to identify any gaps your superstars may have. Are the objectives they're suggesting pointing toward your goals, or are they misunderstanding your longer-range plan?
3. It empowers your team members to make their own meaningful contributions. Your superstars are far from your competitors' typical rank-and-file drones; they have a voice that actually

contributes, which frees you up for more higher-level strategic thinking.

This type of multidirectional conversation is one of the primary missing ingredients in most PM programs. It's also the primary reason SBOs are trapped being the chief doers in their business. Many SBOs are far too busy doing the work to step back and off the treadmill to think about how to strategically engage their team.

When superstars are not strategically engaged, they get bored and find engagement elsewhere. Ironically, when SBOs mismanage this process *they* create high turnover, which buries them that much deeper in the daily grind. In other words, you may have been the one who dug the hole you or your superstar fell in. As British politician Denis Healey once said, "If you find yourself in a hole—stop digging."

Objective-Setting Success Factor #3: Have Your Superstars Send Objectives in Advance

A third way to focus your mutual objective-setting meeting is to have superstars send their objectives in advance. That way you can catch a glimpse of their perspectives before you begin your meeting, allowing you extra time to tweak or redirect the conversation.

Objective-Setting Success Factor #4: Create a Superstar Support Folder

Finally, I recommend you create and use a superstar support folder. The purpose of the folder is for you to collect notes about each superstar throughout each quarter that might support their development. You'll refer to this folder before your monthly one-on-one meetings and when writing quarterly appraisals.

You will actually need two folders: one physical and one digital. The former might be nothing more than a basic manila-type folder stored in your filing system. The latter could be an email or other digital subfolder. Both serve the same function of holding performance indicators about your superstars throughout the quarter.

You may already have some kind of personnel folder in a file cabinet drawer—but what's really in that thing? Is it fresh, current, and alive—or dusty and dying? If you don't have a superstar support folder, you'll be stuck trying to remember everything that happened throughout the quarter, and we have already demonstrated why that's a bad idea.

Here are some items you might include in a superstar support folder:

- Accolades from customers, vendors, and others about your superstars
- Saved emails or physical reports for coaching purposes (reporting errors, harsh language, faulty logic, etc.)
- Relevant status reports
- Thoughts, ideas, or coaching opportunities you noted

This kind of folder is a basic, but critical, piece of a world-class PM process. By having one, you can ensure your feedback during quarterly check-ins is current, functionally organized, and—best of all—always ready. Your superstar support folders can help you focus your feedback. Focused feedback empowers your superstars to do better work. The better they work, the better you sleep at night.

Let's fast forward, assuming you had a great initial objective-setting conversation. Now you have to document those objectives and check back in with your superstars on what progress they made toward achieving them.

Step 2: 30-Day Conversation

After a using a collaborative approach in your initial quarterly objective setting, get out of the way (see Figure 9.3 on page 128). Let your superstars make their way. As they go, take good notes. Notice what they do. Notice what they don't do. This process doesn't have to be anything elaborate. You just need useful material for your first 30-day check-in, which is critical to the success of this PM process. Here are a few guidelines that could help make your first conversation productive.

Figure 9.3—The 30-Day Conversation

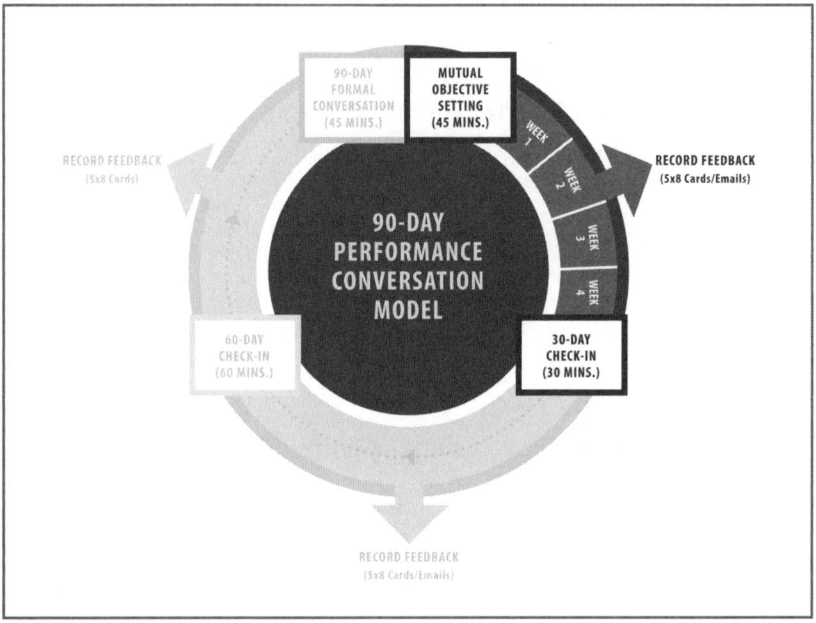

Review the Initial Mutual Objectives

Take notes throughout the month about your superstar's performance. You could simply take 60 seconds a few times per month, just to jot down a note or two about your superstar's performance. That way you're not rushing to think of things five minutes prior to check-ins, which would not be fair to your superstar.

Here's where your superstar support folder comes in handy. Prior to the first check-in, review the mutual objectives you initially set. Refresh your memory of the goals and objectives you both agreed upon. That way you're clear about the issues and don't waste valuable one-on-one time getting caught up.

Three Statements Your Superstar Could Make During Check-Ins

Not only do PM conversations often get hurt by poor timing, but lack of focus can also hijack them. How can you ensure your 30-day check-ins are optimally focused? What can you do to offer the most appropriate feedback in the most efficient manner? There are actually three statements both you and your superstar can make to guarantee you hit the feedback bull's-eye. Let's start by looking at statements your superstar can make.

Check-in Statement #1: Here's What's Not Green (and Why)

One of my favorite approaches for receiving status updates is the simple stoplight approach (see Figure 9.4):

- **Red (R)** = stop—on hold, not currently moving forward
- **Yellow (Y)** = caution—there could be an issue here
- **Green (G)** = go—everything is fine and on track

Although this particular version of the book you are reading is in shades of black and white, I think you'll get the idea. You can download a free full-color, digital spreadsheet that you can modify from

Figure 9.4—**The Stoplight Status Update Approval**

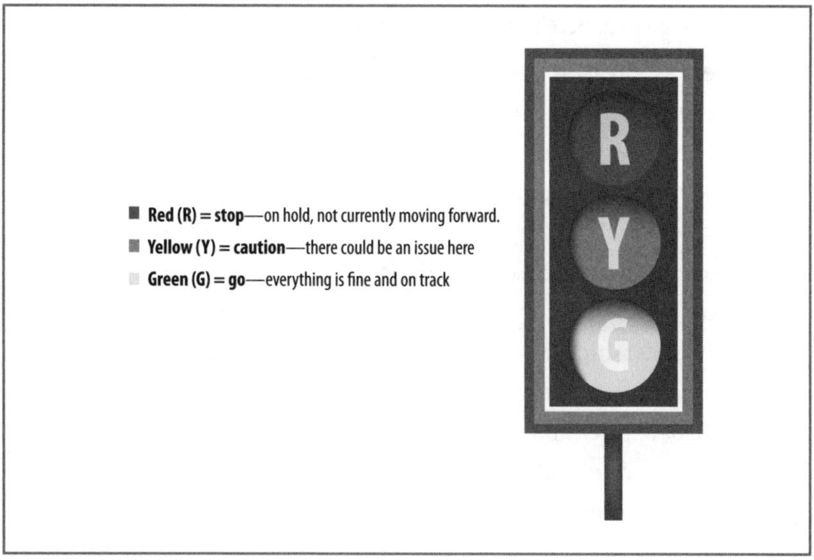
Red (R) = stop—on hold, not currently moving forward.
Yellow (Y) = caution—there could be an issue here
Green (G) = go—everything is fine and on track
R
Y
G

www.christophermcintyre.com. The stoplight approach is useful for the associative minds who prefer a simple, color-coded status update. They are also extremely useful for keeping your 30-day check-ins highly focused.

If you have a core team of superstars chasing clear goals, your leadership could simply be a matter of holding the vision, removing obstacles, and motivating your superstars. That motivation will naturally occur if you remove barriers and simply make it easier for your team to be successful. When it comes to obstacles, though, you must first expect your team to identify them by clarifying what's *not* moving forward appropriately (or green)—and why?

The *why* part of this question is pretty straightforward, but let's touch on the principle behind it. You probably hate to hear "I don't know why it's broke, boss" from someone who's clearly trying to duck ownership of an issue. You're paying them to own issues. Now, if the answer was "I don't know why yet, but I'm trying to figure it out," that's a different story and one that deserves your patience. The principle is that your superstars should never feel comfortable bringing you a problem without also bringing a reason the problem is occurring.

Check-In Statement 2: Here's What I'm Doing About It

The reason *their* reason is important is because it's the thing *they* should use to solve the problem. What are you, the superstar, doing about the problem you found? The question is linked to another important principle: Only present problems when you have some ideas for a solution.

The "here's what I'm doing about it" response may seem obvious, but there's a more strategic function at play. Too many SBOs set themselves up as being the primary solution provider. That traditional top-down leadership approach can be a primary roadblock to long-term freedom and limits the growth, creativity, and accountability of your team. It also inspires laziness on their part and swallows up your energy. The "what I'm doing about it" approach expects superstar ownership and minimizes the potential for consistently saying, "What do *you* think, boss?"

In defense of SBOs who struggle to resist having all the solutions, it might help knowing that there are quite a few good reasons for this behavior. One primary reason points to a critical difference between SBOs and their CEO corporate counterparts. Corporate employees get promoted for solving problems and having solutions. What do your employees get? Usually . . . just busier. As a result, SBOs often set themselves up to have the most solutions, and *employees* let it happen. *Superstars* don't.

Superstar Accountability Principle: It's broke—and here's what I'm doing about it.

In additions, SBOs often don't have the luxury of being able to offer many of the traditional incentives (promotions, financial rewards, flexible hours, etc.) corporate CEOs can. That's a huge part of the unique leadership challenge for every SBO, to actually make sense of and motivate superstars to excel in constantly morphing roles and responsibilities.

In fact, all of Book 2 in the *Roadmap to Freedom* series is dedicated to that very subject (*Leading and Motivating Superstars without Money*). Install a trusted and consistent PM system that systematically engages your superstars and keeps everyone focused on the main things. Then clarifying new roles and systematically motivating your superstars won't be such a crapshoot.

The "here is what I'm doing about it" approach is not meant to give your glory hounds another chance to brag about all the great work they do. It's more intended to ensure your team is not in the habit of pushing tough decisions up the chain. It also helps to minimize the impact of your inner control freak by forcing maximum engagement from your team.

A good status update form (seen in Figure 9.5 on page 132) can also help rescue you from your inner control freak, minimizing the chance for you to meddle. In this way, it empowers your superstars to back you off when necessary, allowing you to focus on other things. It also puts accountability squarely on the shoulders of your superstars and minimizes the opportunity to blame *them, that, or it*.

Figure 9.5—Monthly **Objective Status Update Form**

- **RED (R) = Stop**—on hold, not currently moving forward
- **YELLOW (Y) = Caution**—there could be an issue here
- **GREEN (G) = Go**—everything is fine and on track

30-DAY CHECK-IN: KIARA DIDIT JANUARY 29 (OBJECTIVE STATUS UPDATE)					
STATUS	ANNUAL GOAL	QUARTERLY OBJECTIVE	WHY NOT GREEN?	WHAT I'M DOING ABOUT IT	FIX DATE
R	ROI	Compare last year's training costs with student evals	Training receipts lost during office move	Contacting training firms for duplicates	3/22
Y	New PM	Develop our team's "success formula"	Need everyone to read Chris's book	Developing Cliff Notes of book for team	2/14
G	Grow biz to $20M	Establish two new corporate clients this quarter		Will close contracts with Red Robin by 3/15	3/15
G	*NY Times* Bestseller	Finish research for Chapter 8		Will be finished by end of Feb.	2/28

No, a form doesn't sound like a very sexy thing to have. In fact, your team, like most, probably hates any type of additional structure. Dave Konstantin, the founder of K-Co Construction, even noted it as a joke around his office. He said his team jokes, "I feel a form coming on" every time they don't understand a particular process. But Dave also highlighted the value of formality around key processes.

The status-update form requires specific information from your superstars. It also links relevant company goals directly to your superstar's quarterly objectives. That's a very important link to consistently make. How is what we're talking about linked to our goals? In this way, you can ensure your bigger-picture goals remain the ultimate priority.

While the yellow and the red areas are critical to discuss during your check-ins, be sure not to focus solely on them. Reporting on the green areas gives your superstars a chance to shine and allows you some good news along with the never-ending challenges.

Psychologically, the green items will give you the boost of energy you need to deal with the yellows and reds. Green items will also help you and your superstars stay calibrated on what's right in your world.

A green, yellow, and red update approach offers simple vocabulary that you can easily build into the fabric of your culture. But when you devise a status update form for your business, involving your team is almost always a winning tactic. You may find it useful to chat with your superstars about the basic elements they think would be most useful for this kind of status update form.

Check-In Statement 3: Here's Where I Need Your Help

The first two check-in statements are all about expecting your superstars to own all the issues related to their performance. There's still one final, quick, laser-focused statement for them to answer, but this one is about you: What can *you* do for *them?* Without fail, one of the questions the very best leaders consistently ask is: "Where do you need my help?"

Where do your superstars want you to be? Consider Figure 9.4 when receiving feedback from your team. Expect your superstars to directly ask:

- Could you *start* _____________ so I can ____________________?
- Could you *stop* ______________ so I can ____________________?
- Could you *continue* ___________ so I can ____________________?

Start: Hey boss, could you *start* delegating more of the Cable Business Services work so *I* can develop a better relationship with their sales team?"

In the above, you are encouraging very direct language for a reason here. First, it empowers your superstars. Encouraging direct language creates trust and improves communication. By expecting superstars to speak up about their needs, you empower accountability. By linking their requests to the business case, you're asking them to demonstrate that they understand the impact of their actions on the goals.

Stop: Hey boss, could you *stop* dropping off last-minute noncritical tasks, like updating the database, so *I* can focus on more important work like the Canadian proposal?

One of the biggest gaps in leadership today is because SBOs often fail to ask the most important question of all: Tell me—the boss—what I need to *stop* doing in order to help you better accomplish your objectives. Wow—how empowering. How ego-free. How necessary. It is very possible that you are doing things you *think* are useful that may not be. Ask. Listen. *Stop.*

Continue: Hey boss, I'd love for you to *continue* letting me run the staff meetings, so *I* can establish myself more as a leader on the team.

Lastly, ask what is something *I am doing* that is working for you? By encouraging answers to that question directly, you can confirm what things you're doing that work for each superstar. This is important for you to know, not guess about. Hearing it directly from someone else identifies the path of least resistance. Keep traveling it.

Hitting the bull's-eye with each of your superstars by consistently responding to these three statements will add substantial focus to your feedback sessions. It will also help everyone become more fully engaged. You might be thinking, "Well, what if I can't start, stop, or continue doing what they've asked me?" Answer: No problem—admit it to your employee and, wherever possible, provide a real reason.

Be honest about your choices when responding to feedback and always link your own answers to a business outcome. Make sure your superstars know you're not just dismissing their inputs, even if you can't act on them. If your team genuinely feels heard, they will usually respect your choices. If they don't, well, now it's your turn to give a little feedback.

Three Statements You Should Make During Check-Ins

As you've seen, part of the responsibility for having productive check-in conversations resides with your superstars—and part of the responsibility is also yours. You can make three simple statements to efficiently hit the bull's-eye for your monthly check-ins.

When it comes to you *giving* superstars feedback during the 30-day check-in, the *start, stop, continue* approach may not work as well. Think about it. Suggesting "here's what you need to start doing" is pretty harsh. In fact, it's probably too harsh. When you *invite* that kind of direct language, it's empowering. When you give it, it could be intimidating.

There's a way to convey the exact same information without the harsh language. See if you can find the "start, stop, continue" among the following questions :

- ➡ A *little more* __________ might really help us to ______________
- ➡ A *little less* ________________ could __________________________
- ➡ I *liked* the way you ___________, it really helped ______________

More: Hey Kiara, a little *more* focus on cold calls this month *might* help us to get new customers into the sales funnel.

In this instance you're subtly asking Kiara if she could *start* making more calls *because* sales aren't where they need to be.

Less: I think a little *less* hanging around the water cooler before and after lunch *could* help minimize the distractions for the rest of our office staff.

What you're saying here is *stop* wasting time around the water coolers *because* you're bugging other workers.

Like: I *liked* the way you dealt with Regina and Anne's disagreement about the cupcake issue. It really *helped* to get them focused on the Canadian contract again.

What you're saying is, *continue* handling the office drama, it's *improving* the Canadian contract issues.

You probably get the point here. Start. Stop. Continue. More. Less. Like. However you need to get that information, get it. If you've got a super-close office where everyone's 100 percent candid in their communication, then by all means–be candid.

Be warned, though. I've seen many misperceptions here. SBOs often believe they've got a relationship with their team that supports direct corrective communication. The problem is that 95 percent of that "corrective" communication is one way–from the top down. Such lopsided communications usually breed a hostile environment.

One final warning: It takes courage and skill to accept and deliver personalized critical feedback. It may not be easy to do at first, especially because you must resist the urge to retaliate against your team when they give you feedback you don't want to hear or act on. You can make receiving critical feedback easier by doing it more often. Be sure, though, to capture the feedback you get and give.

Review Your 5-by-8 Notes

One great method of capturing performance notes is the "5-by-8 method." Dig up a couple of 5-by-8 index cards. On one side, you will write down the feedback you receive. The other is for the feedback you give. It's easy to keep up the 5-by-8 method, and best of all, it's personal and tailored. During your session, be sure to jot down the "more, less, liked" feedback you gave.

There's a tactical reason you may actually want to handwrite your 5-by-8 card. When was the last time you received a handwritten letter from someone? I'll bet it was a while ago. We're so busy in the digital age that sometimes we forget the personal impact our feedback has. Your feedback sessions might become more sincere, focused, personal, and effective if you slow down, reflect, and handwrite.

Figure 9.6 shows an example of what you might write on each side of the 5-by-8 card.

A multidirectional feedback approach like this one requires you to listen and ask personal as well as professional questions. Chances are

Figure 9.6—**Capture Feedback You Give on a 5 x 8 Card**

Front Side *January 29th* *Personal Monthly Update—Kiara Didit* *Son 14 (Frankie) nervous about 1st prom.* *Daughter 16 (Aimee)—playing basketball this year in high school (varsity)* *Husband (Mike)—just lost his job (again . . .) Crazy Mother in law—in town for month (do you need to be rescued?)*	*Back Side* *January 29th* *Professional Monthly Update—Kiara Didit* *More: Cold calls (sales are low)* *Less: Folks hanging around the water cooler before and after lunch (distracting others)* *Liked: Handling argument between Regina & Anne. (got them focused again quickly—thank you)*

you're already hearing about most of this stuff anyway. Why not just write it down a couple times a month and check later on it? By checking on the personal stuff, you remind your superstars that their well-being is also part of the "bottom line" you care about.

Step 3: 60-Day Conversation

The 60-day conversation is easy (see Figure 9.7). You're simply repeating the 30-day process, with one very important addition: check-ins. You're pulling up the 5-by-8 index cards and asking how you did over the past 30 days addressing the issues that came up in the feedback session during the last check-in.

Remember your *start, stop, continue* part of the agreement? There's only one thing worse than not checking in with your superstars: checking in, agreeing to change, and then ignoring your agreements.

Figure 9.7—**The 60-Day Conversation**

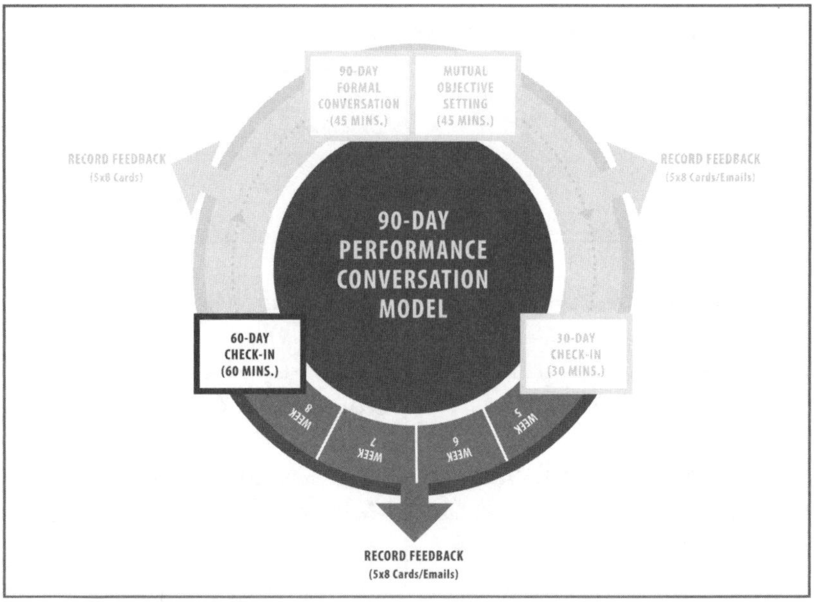

Don't do that—unless you want to destroy your team's trust in you and in your PM process.

Most people have an amazing memory when it comes to remembering instances you didn't do what you said you would. Making the time to review previous feedback before discussing how to move forward is a very simple way to ensure your team knows they're being heard. Figure 9.8 gives you an example of how to check in on the feedback you received from your superstar.

Before we get into the final 90-day evaluation, here's a word of caution about the 60-day conversation. Watch your timing. You're not just following up with each other's feedback at this point. You're also sharing new insights on how best to move forward for the next 30 to 90 days. For this reason, you may want to allot a little more time for this session.

As a reminder, we'll address timing directly in Chapter 11. Just be sure to keep track of time and ensure your 60-day check-in doesn't

Figure 9.8—**Capture Feedback You Receive on a 5 x 8 Card**

Front Side *Feb 28th (Kiara Didit)* *You said: Start delegating key work:* *1. I gave you the lead on the Small Business Services Account.* *2. I put you in charge of the office maintenance Schedule.* *You said: Stop dropping off last-minute stuff:* *1. I save everything but critical issues for our bi-weekly staff meetings now.*	*Back Side* *Feb 28th (Kiara Didit)* *Stop (cont'd)* *2. I read David Allen's "GTD" book, and now have an "Agenda" list for you (so I don't have to bug you all the time).* *Continue: Letting you run meetings:* *1. Gave you the lead during the weekly staff meetings* *2. Don't get GREEDY—I'm still the boss*

become a dreaded multihour time-waster. Keep it short, simple, and highly focused. That will help to make your 90-day formal evaluations flow easily.

Step 4: 90-Day Formal Conversation

Here it is: the moment of truth. The good news is that because you set clear mutual objectives and made time for frequent performance conversations along the way, your superstars should know exactly where they stand. Unless your superstar has experienced a horrible third month, there should be no surprises when it comes to ratings (see Figure 9.9).

The formal conversation goes hand in hand with the appraisal form we'll discuss in a minute. Before you begin, however, there are a few things you can do to prepare for the evaluation conversation.

Figure 9.9—**The 90-Day Conversation**

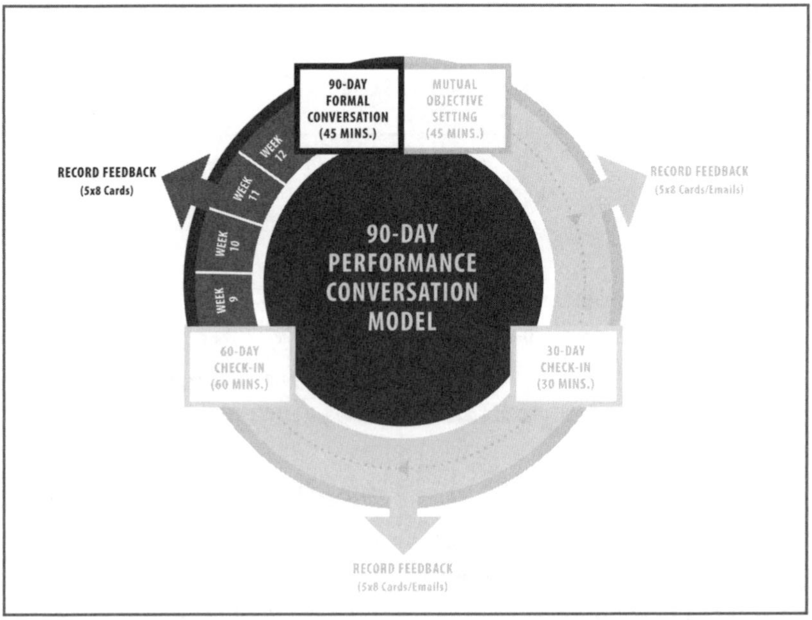

Review the Superstar Support Folder

Go back to your physical and digital folders and review what you've collected throughout the quarter. Familiarize yourself with the objectives your superstars set for themselves during the initial meeting. If your superstars will be coming into their monthly check-ins with the green, yellow, and red status updates, you should have a copy of them too.

Review your 5-by-8 cards and look for any general themes around performance. Review any other information, sticky notes, awards, emails, or other performance reminders you may have collected throughout the quarter. This is where your folder earns it value. Your superstars' entire quarterly performance indicators should already be in there, simply waiting for you to tally.

Assess Your Superstar

It's rating time. How do you present the magic numbers? Did your superstars achieve their quarterly objectives or not? What was missed? What was done exceptionally well and what was just average? This is precisely where your best thinking is needed the most; don't cheat the process. The more effort you put into this moment, the less time you'll spend giving frustrated feedback later.

Dr. Steven Jones is by far one of the very best management consultants I've encountered. I love how he summed up the ratings phase of a strong PM process:

> *By the time it comes to the ratings, it's less about what you're giving your superstars and more about what they've earned.*

I couldn't agree more. When you have a clean, trusted PM program in place, this process is no longer a wildly subjective "in the moment" judgment call. You've got measurable objectives your superstar and you both agreed upon. You have your 5-by-8 cards and all the other information you have collected in the personnel folder.

Have Superstars Bring Their Self-Assessments

Have your superstars come to the conversation with their performance evaluation forms filled out in advance. Actually have them rate themselves. This forces them to prepare for your conversation too. Since you will also have your take on their ratings, it also helps sharpen the conversation by identifying gaps between your perceptions of their performance.

Let your superstars take the lead. How did they rate themselves and why? Do they have specific examples of what they've done? Are they consistently focusing on your long-range goals? Just listen and stay focused. Then, when it's time for dialogue, target the gaps.

Focus on the Gaps

As a peak-performance speaker and SBO consultant, I can say without a doubt that many of the issues that negatively impact teams revolve around similar themes. Disagreements about what constitutes "excellent" performance are very common in a wide variety of businesses. When it comes to "excellent" performance, there are almost always gaps between what the superstar and SBO think.

For example, if a superstar rates himself low in a certain area when you rated him high, there's a gap in perception. It could be that the superstar isn't aware how well you believe he's performing. If he doesn't know how much you value his performance, he may stop trying so hard, which could reverse his positive performance.

Of course, the opposite situation is far worse. There are times when a superstar rates herself high in a certain area when you saw her recent performance as less productive. This type of gap is extremely important to identify early on so you can get on the same page with the superstar and correct the issue before it spirals into a major problem. By having the discussion at this stage, you are also sending an indirect signal to the team that declining performance gets noticed.

This gap-checking process minimizes miscommunication, but you should never expect 100 percent agreement. That's actually a good thing. Differences in perspective create a good type of friction. Good friction promotes candid dialogue and points to opportunities for growth for both you and your superstar. Bad friction, on the other hand, is typically due to unclear goals, objectives, expectations, and/or vague rating and communication systems.

The next chapter will show you exactly how to strategically create, isolate, and make the most of good friction–and eliminate most of that bad friction.

Figure 9.10—Chapter 9 Summary Checklist: The Quarterly Conversation

OUTCOME	RATING
Strongly Agree	6
Agree	5
Somewhat Agree	4
Somewhat Disagree	3
Disagree	2
Strongly Disagree	1
KEY STATEMENTS	**RATING**
Checkpoint #1: I empower multidirectional planning and feedback systems.	
a. I have clear goals for my business.	
b. I distinguish between larger goals and shorter objectives.	
c. My superstars see how their objectives are directly connected to our goals.	
d. I involve my superstars in much of my longer-range goal-setting processes.	
e. I empower my superstars to share in objective-setting conversations.	
Checkpoint #2: I have a lean, hyper-focused, feedback process in place for monthly performance check-ins.	
a. I expect "start, stop, continue" feedback from my team.	
b. I give focused, sensitive "more, less, liked" feedback.	
c. I understand feedback is personal and give myself time to tailor it.	
d. No one on my team brings problems without some idea for forward movement.	
e. I have clear forms and structures around key processes.	
Checkpoint #3: I have an excellent performance management system in place that I actually use and trust.	
a. I install accountability by expecting superstars to ask for what they need.	
b. I use some kind of superstar support folders to help me give relevant feedback.	
c. I specifically target gaps in perspective when formally discussing feedback.	
d. I welcome the good friction of differing perspectives about performance.	
e. My superstars trust that I genuinely care about them—personally and professionally.	

Figure 9.10—**Chapter 9 Summary Checklist: The Quarterly Conversation,** continued

Actions I could take to improve my current 1-on-1 performance conversations:
a.
b.
c.
d.
e.

Chapter 10

The Connection

In many ways, a successful PM performance management (PM) program comes down to the documentation of a well-spent conversation. Documentation, like problem solving, is easy when you ask the right questions. This chapter is all about connecting and aligning the right people to the right message in the right way at the right time. Before we look at the form, let's define a key term that affected how it was developed.

The Knowledge Worker

In the late 1960s, Peter Drucker wrote a book called *The Effective Executive* (HarperCollins, 2006) in which he discussed a primary shift in the type of work that was being done in industrial societies. He distinguished between traditional *manual workers* and emerging *knowledge workers* in ways that are illustrated in Figure 10.1 on page 148.

As an example, workers in fast-food chains are considered *manual workers* because they have work to do that's rigidly

Figure 10.1—Manual Workers vs. Knowledge Workers

MANUAL WORKERS	KNOWLEDGE WORKERS
Standardized work	Dynamic work
Work is predefined	Work must be defined
Labor is primary asset	Knowledge is primary asset
Focus is on efficiency	Focus is on effectiveness

defined for them. They push the same buttons. They make the same burgers. They wait for three minutes every time for the fries to be done. They squeeze the same amount of mustard, mayo, and ketchup onto the burger. Basically, they repeat the same predefined actions over and over again. In order for fast-food workers to be successful, they typically just have to follow the process and move quickly and efficiently.

Compare that manual work to the type of work you do on a daily basis. Your primary function, as a *knowledge worker*, is to define your work. There's no easy button to push. No burgers to flip. With minimal structure to guide your day, there's an infinite number of ineffective ways you could spend your time. Unlike that of most manual workers, your effectiveness hinges on decisive insight that aligns actions with constantly shifting priorities.

Understanding the knowledge worker concept is critical to your PM process for two reasons: (1) As an SBO, you are a knowledge worker; and (2) you probably lead knowledge workers. You have to measure your superstars' ability to do work that hasn't shown up yet. You're not just counting the burgers (or outputs) they produce.

Much of the important work your superstars do lurks in the gray space without an immediately measurable result to count, smell, touch, or taste. In other words, your PM program has to make visible the invisible knowledge work. A good PM form like the one in Figure 10.2 on page 149 can help you make that happen.

The Full Form

Let's start by looking at the full form, and then we can break it down, piece by piece, and discuss it. The full, pretty form wouldn't fit neatly into this book. I would encourage you to take a minute, go to my website (www.christophermcintyre.com) and download the free one. It's in a modifiable format, so you can tailor it, and every tool in this book.

Figure 10.2—**The Form**

NAME: KIARA DIDIT	
Rater:	Frankie Havai
Period:	Q 1—2013
Team:	Sales
SECTION I: OUR OUTCOMES	**RATINGS**
Exceeded standards for every objective	5
Exceeded standards for most objectives	4
Exceeded some and / or met standards for all objectives	3
Met standards for some objectives	2
Should make an impact for our competition's team immediately	1

Figure 10.2—The Form, continued

SECTION II: OUR MOST VALUABLE ASSETS			
MVAs (Who)	**ANNUAL GOALS (Why)**	**QUARTERLY OBJECTIVES (What)**	**RATING (How)**
C U S T O M E R	Grow the business to $20M this year	Establish two new large corporate clients (determined by superstar) (listen for gaps)	5 4 3 2 1
P R O D U C T	Calculate Return on Investment for all sales training last year	Compare last year's training costs with student evaluations (determined by superstar) (listen for gaps)	5 4 3 2 1
T E A M	Get a performance management system in place by end of year	Develop our team's systematic success formula (determined by superstar) (listen for gaps)	5 4 3 2 1
F I N A N C E	Cut advertising costs by 25%	Put together a social media marketing campaign (determined by superstar) (listen for gaps)	5 4 3 2 1

Figure 10.2—**The Form,** continued

SECTION III: OUR SYSTEMATIC SUCCESS FORMULA: ENGAGE	RATING
What: Defines Success ➡ Defines what success looks like now ➡ Defines what success does not look like now ➡ Clarifies what needs to be done and how to do it ➡ Identifies opportunities for success we can control **How:** (to be led by superstar) (listen for gaps . . .)	5 4 3 2 1
What: Prepares for Success ➡ Burns the midnight oil ➡ Practices deliberate ignorance ➡ Leans into mistakes ➡ Deals with wild fluctuation **How:** (to be led by the superstar) (listen for gaps . . .)	5 4 3 2 1
What: Creates Opportunities for Success ➡ Finds ways to be of use ➡ Welcomes the Weiji ➡ Burns the right bridges ➡ Publishes useful failures **How:** (to be led by the superstar) (listen for gaps . . .)	5 4 3 2 1
What: Takes Action ➡ Readily offers and acts on the next action ➡ Doesn't let failures confuse the vision ➡ Lowers the bar at times ➡ Is never OK with OK **How:** (to be led by the superstar) (listen for gaps . . .)	5 4 3 2 1

Figure 10.2—The Form, continued

SECTION IV: OUR DISCUSSION (RATE THE BOSS)	RATING
Start:	5
	4
	3
	2
	1
Stop:	5
	4
	3
	2
	1
Continue:	5
	4
	3
	2
	1

SECTION IV: OUR DISCUSSION (THOUGHTS FOR SUPERSTAR)	RATING
More:	5
	4
	3
	2
	1
Less:	5
	4
	3
	2
	1
Liked:	5
	4
	3
	2
	1

Figure 10.2—**The Form,** continued

SECTION V: SUMMARY NOTES

______________________ ______________________________
Date Signed/Superstar

______________________ ______________________________
Date Signed/SBO

The Form: Logistics

Let's start at the top of the form with logistics. This is pretty straightforward.

Figure 10.3—The Basic Logistics

NAME: KIARA DIDIT	
Rater:	Frankie Havai
Period:	Q 1—2013
Team:	Sales

This is where you input the basic logistical information you need. You'll want the name of the superstar being rated, along with the rater. Specify the department and other useful logistical information. Notice there is no "date delivered" block. The sign and date stamp on the last page is meant to be left blank until the day the conversation actually happens.

The Form: Section I—Outcomes and Ratings

The ratings and outcomes are critical parts of the form. Section I (Figure 10.4 on page 155) is primarily where most PM programs get ugly. Typically you'll see very vague (Excellent, Good, Fair, Poor) outcomes that are highly subjective and are left up to the rater to determine. In fact, take a look at your current PM form if you have one and see if it's clear and distinct. See any room for ambiguity? Here are a few simple things you can do to ensure your form is clearly understood.

Separate "Outcomes" from "Ratings"

First, consider separating the outcomes (end results) from the ratings (or rank)—even though they are linked. By separating outcomes from ratings you can discuss both independently with your team before rolling them out. The outcomes and ratings deserve distinct and separate focus because of the highly emotional impact they generate

Figure 10.4—**Outcomes and Ratings**

SECTION I: OUR OUTCOMES	RATINGS
Exceeded standards for every objective	5
Exceeded standards for most objectives	4
Exceeded some and / or met standards for all objectives	3
Met standards for some objectives	2
Should make an impact for our competition's team immediately	1

once connected. It's also a nice place to involve your superstars, given its sensitive nature.

Depending on the business culture you're trying to craft, you may prefer not using a hard number ratings system. I've seen lots of teams get hung up on the ratings, regardless of what the outcomes suggested. You might prefer to have the "best" outcome be the lowest number (1) instead of the highest number (5). Perhaps your team struggles with the idea of a (3) being the average number that most people will receive. They may prefer a traditional (A, B, C, D) school-style rating system instead. Go with what works for you and your team.

Remove Gray Space between Outcomes

Remember the "bad friction" of the gaps we discussed earlier? One of the biggest reasons for dissent around PM programs is that the outcomes often seem vague. What does "excellent" mean to you? Where's the line between good and excellent performance? Gray space between outcomes opens the door for confusion and disagreement. Clear and measureable outcomes help to remove that gray space. Look at the outcomes in Figure 10.4. There's no room for disagreement.

Do you see the difference between (5) exceeding standards for *every* objective and (4) exceeding *most*? There is no room for someone to feel slighted if she met all standards but only (3) exceeded some. Even someone who meets most standards but struggles in (2) a few areas can't argue. Then of course, there's the (1) team member who needs an immediate evacuation. Let's give that superstar the tools to sink your competition's ship as soon as possible.

You can modify this entire scale however you wish. If you've gone through the process highlighted in the first chapter, super-low performers will be a rarity. But let's face it, sometimes superstars make the choice to morph into nightmares.

In this way, when it comes time to hit the eject button for your nightmares, it won't be a surprise to them. It won't be a debatable situation, either. You'll never have to worry about the "big bad boss fires a poor undeserving victim" scenario again. That is, unless your victim's absolutely insane. In that case, this book won't help you one bit. Grab your favorite Holy Book and seek more guidance.

The Form: Section II—Our Most Valuable Assets

Your most valuable assets (MVAs) are the key assets that matter most to the success of your business. What, or who, must every individual focus on and contribute to? Consistent neglect of any one of those critical elements could mean bad news for your business.

Your MVAs will typically be your:

- Customers
- Products (or services)
- Team
- Finances

You may want to add different MVAs, and that's fine. In fact, that's a key point of this entire book. Clarify your own MVAs using the four above as an example. You can stick with these or tailor them as necessary. The important thing in Section II of the form is to directly connect the goals for your business with your employees' quarterly objectives. Both the goals and objectives should point directly to the MVAs.

Sections II and III of the PM form are where you formally connect every individual with every most important business objectives, so it's critical for you to measure the right things. Remember in Part I we saw that there was no right way to hit the wrong target. There's nothing more demoralizing to a superstar than achieving the wrong objectives.

Here are four very basic questions for you to link when supporting your MVAs:

1. **Who** are we supporting, or which MVA is this aligned with?
2. **Why** are we doing this, or which annual goal is this supporting?
3. **What** are the quarterly objectives that will get us closer to the goal?
4. **How** well were those quarterly objectives achieved?

These four questions help you keep the bigger picture in mind while providing focus for action-oriented conversations with your superstars. They also help you to listen for gaps in how your superstars understand their role in reaching the larger-picture goals. Finally, perhaps most importantly, this approach expects the superstars to share accountability for the success of the business goals. This is bottom-up leadership at its finest.

Figure 10.6 on page 159 shows how you can connect your superstar's quarterly objectives directly to goals supporting the business's most valuable assets.

Let's stick with the same goals and objectives we used earlier in the mutual objective-setting conversation. To keep the examples simple, there is only one objective per goal. You will probably have more. Your superstars might have several objectives during any one quarter, based on how aggressive they are.

In Figure 10.5 on page 158, notice the big-to-small flow built right into the PM form.

The form ties MVAs (that rarely change) and your (annual) business goals directly to your superstars' (quarterly) objectives, which are assessed by a very specific rating. That deliberate linkage helps your

Figure 10.5—Link MVAs, Goals, and Objectives

SECTION II: OUR MOST VALUABLE ASSETS			
MVAs (Who)	**ANNUAL GOALS (Why)**	**QUARTERLY OBJECTIVES (What)**	**RATING (How)**
CUSTOMER	Grow the business to $20M this year	Establish two new large corporate clients (determined by superstar) (listen for gaps)	5 4 3 2 1
PRODUCT	Calculate Return on Investment for all sales training last year	Compare last year's training costs with student evaluations (determined by superstar) (listen for gaps)	5 4 3 2 1
TEAM	Get a performance management system in place by end of year	Develop our team's systematic success formula (determined by superstar) (listen for gaps)	5 4 3 2 1
FINANCE	Cut advertising costs by 25%	Put together a social media marketing campaign (determined by superstar) (listen for gaps)	5 4 3 2 1

Figure 10.6—**Connecting Who, Why, What, and How**

SECTION II: OUR MOST VALUABLE ASSETS			
MVAs (Who)	ANNUAL GOALS (Why)	QUARTERLY OBJECTIVES (What)	RATING (How)

superstars keep performance conversations focused on the right things. It also creates space for your superstars to actually create, and take ownership for, their own quarterly objectives.

Author Stephen Covey summed up this point well when he said, "The main thing is to keep the main thing the main thing." A form like this helps you to do just that. In this way, you can ensure every single individual (from janitor to COO) in your business sees how she's contributing to the business's main things.

Here's the key to this approach. You develop the annual goals and focus the strategic direction for your business on protecting your MVAs. Your superstars take your goals and create their own quarterly objectives. Give them as much space as you're comfortable with. Remember, you went through all that rigor earlier to get top talent on board. Now it's time to expect them to prove that you made the right choice in bringing them on.

Connecting your business goals and your superstars' objectives to your MVAs is leading-edge stuff, but it's only part of what a true world-class PM program does. One more critical element is still necessary for alignment, if you really want a true *Roadmap to Freedom*. We still have to install *the core* message–your systematic success formula.

The Form: Section III—Our Systematic Success Formula

You didn't think you were going to do all that hard work, in Part II of the book, of figuring out your systematic success formula for nothing, did you? I hope not. This is where the real magic happens.

Not only is your systematic success formula the secret sauce most SBOs ignore, but by connecting it directly to your PM program, you can help hard-wire the intuition of your superstars. Highlighting this key formula enables you to systematically guide all actions so you can expect—and actually install—more consistency in your team's performance.

Your MVAs rarely change. Your goals change every year or two. However, the fundamental elements of your success formula stay pretty much the same. That's important and deliberate. Since they don't change often, you can rely on them to serve as deep anchors and values that guide all actions. In this way, you can install the key PEAs that guide actions on a daily and quarterly basis.

What does change frequently, however, is *how* your superstars will use the success formula every quarter given your current business goals. Figure 10.7 on page 161 shows how to install your success formula into your PM program.

The more your superstars contribute—and get measured on—your success formula, the more they'll own it. How can your superstars apply the formula this quarter? One simple way to find out: Ask them! If your success formula principles are solid, your business will always need them in some way.

What's going on in your business now? Should the team focus more on *creating* opportunities or *acting* on them? Perhaps they should actually stop taking so much *action* and spend a little more time actually *defining* what success might look like. This is where you enable your superstars to own valuable contributions to the needs of the business.

This is the *core* message for "how" things can consistently get done. Tailor away. This piece of the form is all about installing a consistent mantra about your key PEAs. It's meant to keep every individual on the team performing in a way that will ruthlessly protect, and thoroughly promote, the business brand. Involve your team in how you might break that mantra down into distinct elements (your formula) that can be measured.

Think less. Ask more. This PM approach deliberately challenges the traditional top-down (boss knows best) objective-setting model

Figure 10.7—**Our Systematic Success Formula**

SECTION III: OUR SYSTEMATIC SUCCESS FORMULA: ENGAGE	RATING
What: Defines Success ➡ Defines what success looks like now ➡ Defines what success does not look like now ➡ Clarifies what needs to be done and how to do it ➡ Identifies opportunities for success we can control **How:** (to be led by superstar) (listen for gaps . . .)	5 4 3 2 1
What: Prepares for Success ➡ Burns the midnight oil ➡ Practices deliberate ignorance ➡ Leans into mistakes ➡ Deals with wild fluctuation **How:** (to be led by the superstar) (listen for gaps . . .)	5 4 3 2 1
What: Creates Opportunities for Success ➡ Finds ways to be of use ➡ Welcomes the Weiji ➡ Burns the right bridges ➡ Publishes useful failures **How:** (to be led by the superstar) (listen for gaps . . .)	5 4 3 2 1
What: Takes Action ➡ Readily offers and acts on the next action ➡ Doesn't let failures confuse the vision ➡ Lowers the bar at times ➡ Is never OK with OK **How:** (to be led by the superstar) (listen for gaps . . .)	5 4 3 2 1

by empowering superstars from the bottom up. The simple, and consistent, question you should ask is: How can I help "you" do what I very clearly expect?

Notice in Figure 10.7, those two very key questions are built directly into the PM form:

1. **What** = Here is what I expect, it's clear, and relevant to our MVAs.
2. **How** = Will you achieve it this quarter? I will guide your answers, but I expect you to know enough about what we're doing here to answer this question intelligently.

You may feel a bit nervous about how much space to give your superstars in sharing such a multidirectional accountability process. Start slow. Trust your gut. Let your superstars know this is new for you, too, and that it might be a challenge for you at first. By publishing your failures along the way, you can articulate what's working and what's not. This will soon feel less like a procedural chore, and more like a simple dialogue and business as usual.

There's still one more risky section left: *your* rating.

The Form: Section IV—Our Discussion (Rate the Boss)

Section IV (shown in Figure 10.8 on page 163) of the form encourages just that. Let your superstars assess *you*. Here you compile all the *start, stop, continue*, and incorporate the *more, less, like* feedback you collected during your monthly check-ins.

Think about the logic here for a minute. If you put all that effort into getting the right high-caliber group of superstars on board, why would you *not* consistently give yourself the gift of their feedback? It's free consulting from some of the finest minds on the planet.

Have you ever heard of the Navy's Blue Angels? They travel around the world

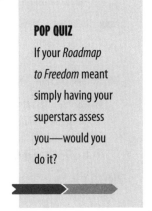

> **POP QUIZ**
> If your *Roadmap to Freedom* meant simply having your superstars assess you—would you do it?

demonstrating amazing precision flying formations and aeronautical movements. These pilots are the very best on the planet–albeit, perhaps, a little insane. They debrief after *every* single event, *every single time*. Guess who leads the group in an egoless debrief critiquing themselves and then demands candid feedback from the group about his performance? Yep, you guessed it: Blue Angel #1, the lead pilot.

Rate yourself about how responsive you think you were to your superstars' requests. They will also fill out this information on you. Be honest. Listen for gaps. This information can offer you

Figure 10.8—**Our Discussions**

<table>
<tr><th>SECTION IV: OUR DISCUSSION (RATE THE BOSS)</th><th>RATING</th></tr>
<tr><td rowspan="5">Start:
➡ Delegating more (especially around key clients)
• I handed off the big Pez contract
• Gave you the lead on the Canadian deal
➡ Team building for leadership team
• Brought in "Be Legendary" team for the Building a Dream Program
➡ Hired J&A for 360-degree leadership assessments</td><td>5</td></tr>
<tr><td>4</td></tr>
<tr><td>3</td></tr>
<tr><td>2</td></tr>
<tr><td>1</td></tr>
<tr><td rowspan="5">Stop:
➡ Withholding sensitive business information
• Started having biweekly "how's it" meetings
• Now sharing all the financials with leadership team</td><td>5</td></tr>
<tr><td>4</td></tr>
<tr><td>3</td></tr>
<tr><td>2</td></tr>
<tr><td>1</td></tr>
<tr><td rowspan="5">Continue:
➡ Having these types of sincerely open PM discussions
• I'm reading Chris's second book about motivating the team—they just keep getting better . . . ☺</td><td>5</td></tr>
<tr><td>4</td></tr>
<tr><td>3</td></tr>
<tr><td>2</td></tr>
<tr><td>1</td></tr>
</table>

rich information about improving your leadership style, which will ultimately give you a more empowered team and more freedom. It also lets your superstars know that they can expect your very best in a raw and vulnerable way.

That said, this approach is also a subtle ethics test. Do your superstars try to manipulate your willingness to be vulnerable? Silently thank them if they do because they're pulling their own ejection cord. They're making themselves easy targets if and when it comes time to let nightmares go. Trust your gut when deciding how much feedback to invite here.

As the SBO, you're Blue Angel #1. Can you name any high-caliber team that doesn't give very candid, timely, and useful multidirectional feedback constantly? The Blue Angels don't give critical feedback while they're flying. They do it in the right place, in the right time, in the right way.

By creating a culture that embraces feedback, at every level, you enlist the entire team in the process. That minimizes backbiting and negative rumor mills because everyone will have a time and place to speak candidly. When that happens, you will no longer be the only one policing things that aren't right. Your team will police itself.

As a reminder, just because they've asked you to do something doesn't mean you actually can or will. Make clear agreements about what you will change, what you won't, and why. If you feel this section is altogether too risky—don't use it.

Modify the form however you wish. The bigger point here is to ensure your superstars feel like their feedback is being heard. If they do, the fruit of your ego-checking labor will be an engaged superstar who owns the vision of your business just as fiercely as you do.

Asking for *start, stop, continue* feedback—and actually doing something with it—will elevate your leadership to a rare status. But following up quarterly regarding what you agreed to change and asking your superstars to assess how you did with their feedback, well, that's *world-class*. Gut check time. Are you willing to risk being world-class?

The Form: Section V—Summary Notes

The final section, summary notes, is another critical piece of the PM form. This is where you summarize the quarterly discussion you had with your superstar. Here you compile the themes you see on your 5-by-8 cards. What might you want to know a year or two from now as you're reviewing old conversations? A larger benefit of this section is to capture the essence of your relationship with each superstar.

How aligned are you with this person? Ask yourself these questions:

- Are you agreeing to more than you're disagreeing to?
- Is your superstar's self-assessment way off track?
- How well do you adjust to each other's feedback?
- How useful is their feedback for you?
- Is this person consistently contributing to the culture you're trying to create?
- Any themes or trends to note?

Fill the summary notes (found in Figure 10.9) out immediately after your conversation and before you run off to your next meeting.

Figure 10.9—**High-Level Summary Notes and Themes**

SECTION V: SUMMARY NOTES
➡ Primarily agreed on the ratings for this quarter. ➡ Had great discussion about how Kiara could get more involved in mentoring Ben, Tom, Doug, and the rest of the younger workers. ➡ Had a bit of disagreement around Kiara being less involved in the team-building events. (She agreed to ask a couple of team members for additional perspectives.) ➡ Kiara's going to reach out to "Be Legendary" folks to get another team-building event on the calendar. ➡ I agreed to delegate even more key projects, depending on how the Canadian contract turns out.

This is another one of those critical areas that deserves your time while the conversation is still fresh in your mind, so capture the Cliff's Notes version of how it went. This high-level info is great for scanning throughout the years to really determine your superstars' overall contributions.

This entire template, and quarterly PM process, is simply meant to improve communication with your team. Consider it a loose framework and make it fit best for you. The *Roadmap to Freedom* requires you to trust that you are clearly and consistently communicating all the key expectations, measures, and feedback processes about what's most important. That's a huge job—so share more of it!

Figure 10.10—**Chapter 10 Summary Checklist: The Connection**

OUTCOME	RATING
Strongly Agree	6
Agree	5
Somewhat Agree	4
Somewhat Disagree	3
Disagree	2
Strongly Disagree	1
KEY STATEMENTS	**RATING**
Checkpoint #1: My performance management (PM) program removes debatable gray space	
a. I realize the significance that knowledge work has on my role as a leader.	
b. My PM program clarifies all key performance indicators.	
c. I clearly distinguish between "outcomes" and "ratings."	
d. I am using outcomes and ratings that fit the culture of my business.	
e. I have worked with my team to get buy-in on my PM system.	
Checkpoint #2: All superstars are directly connected to our most valuable assets (MVAs).	
a. I have clearly identified our most valuable assets.	
b. I communicate how business goals are directly linked to supporting MVAs.	
c. Every superstar understands how she or he contributes to our MVAs.	
d. My PM program distinguishes between who, why, what—and how.	
e. My PM program supports a core message that guides the intuition of my superstars.	
Checkpoint #3: My PM program maximizes multidirectional feedback.	
a. I trust my team enough to have them rate me.	
b. I look for themes in the feedback I receive.	
c. I always check back to see how I've done with feedback from my superstars.	
d. I am diligent in following up on feedback I've given my superstars.	
e. I frequently summarize my superstars' abilities to contribute to the culture I'm trying to create.	

Figure 10.10—Chapter 10 Summary Checklist: The Connection, continued

Actions I could take to improve my performance management process:
a.
b.
c.
d.
e.

Chapter 11

The Rollout

Now that you have a loose template for a world-class performance management program, how do you actually do it? What approach should you use to roll out your program, and how can you get your team involved and sold on the process? Oh yeah, what about that whole "time" issue? Let's finish Book 1 of *The Roadmap to Freedom* series by answering all these pesky, logistical questions.

Rollout Step 1: Getting Buy-In

If you don't already have some kind of PM program in place before rolling out this one, brace yourself: You're probably in for a bumpy ride. Humans usually reject any type of restraint—at least initially. In fact, the higher performing your team is, the more initial friction you can expect. Don't worry, though—it's definitely doable.

Build Your Case

Think about the best way to frame your PM program so that your employees will see it as an intended benefit for the team. One way to do that is to suggest it will be your attempt to empower their feedback about the direction of the business. PM done right is a tool to help you better support the needs of your superstars.

It may seem rare for a superstar to be asked to rate the boss as part of a PM program. This is your opportunity to ask her for a candid perspective about how you can better help her do her job. This is also you expecting your superstar to take even greater ownership of her own objectives. A great PM program clarifies the expectations for your superstars and increases their opportunities to exceed them.

Before soliciting the team's feedback, though, start thinking about your MVAs. What is your systematic success formula? If you don't fully subscribe to a systematic success formula, *per se*, do you have other key competencies or values you'd rather measure? Are you willing to develop them with the team?

To begin to develop the framework, first focus on what you want to achieve with your PM program. What is your intent for implementing this? Worry less about how it should happen at this point. Remember, you don't have to do all the thinking. Let your superstars help with that part.

<u>Here are some framework questions to help build your case:</u>

- What kind of relationships will your team members have with each other?
- How could you verify that the team is optimally engaged?
- Do you have a systematic success formula? What is it?
- What is it you're consistently telling people they should "do" to get better results?
- What are some other key competencies you might be willing to measure?
- Do you have one- to two-year goals? How are they consistently being communicated to your team?
- What level of engagement do you want from your team during this process?

- What kind of resistance might they have about the program? What might your responses be to those issues?

Enlist Your Superstars

At one of your staff meetings, give the group a heads-up on what you're thinking. No need to roll out the details initially–just share your bigger-picture desires, the benefits to them, and your attempt to address *your* personal PM deficiencies (i.e., I want to get better at acting on your feedback). Tell the team you're not sure exactly what it looks like yet, but it will be connected to a new PM program.

Give the team this book to read. Having them read the book is the best way to loosely frame the context for your thinking–and highlight your willingness to empower them. It will also help them to contribute more efficiently to your vision during the rollout.

You might even provide them with a list of questions to be thinking about before you formally introduce your program. If you do give this book to them, be sure to also let them know you will follow up on the program in a couple of weeks. If you don't let them know you'll be revisiting the questions (and then actually do it) in a timely fashion, everyone will think it's just another idea that never got traction.

Here are some questions to help enlist your team:

- What's one word that most describes our culture?
- How do you systematically achieve results?
- What does it take to be successful here?
- What behaviors are not OK here?
- What attributes are most necessary for the success of this business?
- What is it about the culture here that you really appreciate? How could we preserve that? How could we lose that?
- What would you say is the most important soft skill for your job?
- Do you have any cool ideas about how to contribute to this process?

No matter how you do it, be very deliberate about how (and where) you choose to enlist your team in this process. You need to walk the fine line of inviting your team's input while at the same time not losing your true voice along the way. Because you involved them in the early discussion, most superstars will respect your intent and participate fully.

Rollout Step 2: Tailoring the System

Having coached hundreds of SBOs and corporate executives over the years, one thing I've realized is that no one size fits all. That's exactly why this book is meant to be tailored to meet the unique needs of your distinct business. First and foremost, it's your business—and your systematic success mantra. So if you feel strongly about defining all this kind of stuff on your own, have at it. If you feel open to tailor the system with your team's input, here is a potential process to get you started.

Just the exercise on page 173 with your team will be a great way to get them to understand what's most important, in addition to achieving pure results. Another great way you might tailor this process is to modify the formula idea a bit. Instead of taking one simple mantra (such as *engage*), what if you took three to five mantras, defined them, and anchored them to your performance appraisal system? Instead of having define, prepare, create opportunities, and act in Part II of your PM form, perhaps you would have: *Engage, Empathize, Serve, Commit.*

One of the very best resources for well-researched competencies is *Lomingers For Your Improvement (FYI) Guide, 5th Edition* (Lominger Inc., 2009). The Lominger's guide offers over 67 different fully defined competencies (possible mantras) to point you in the right direction. It even offers questions to help guide your PM development conversations. To help get you started though, try working through a few of the mantras in Appendix B.

TEAM ACTIVITY

- Give your team a list of potential mantras found in Appendix B, or download them from www.christophermcintyre.com (and have them feel free to add as they see fit).
- Have everyone choose their top three and explain why they made that choice.
- Bring the team together and put the choices on a wall or flip chart where everyone can see them.
- Identify the top mantras that most people agreed upon (no more than five).
- Have everyone vote until you have one final mantra.
- Give the team a week to develop a "how to do it" (systematic success formula) for your mantra.
- Bring everyone back, share "how" to do it, and then repeat the process above until you have an agreed-upon formula.

Rollout Step 3: Making the Time

I promised we would revisit the time issue. Let's address it directly now by highlighting five time truths.

Time Truth #1: You Make Time for What You Consider Important

As an SBO, you're very busy. Even when you hear great ideas, perhaps you get whisked away by the next issue of the day before you can figure out how best to act on those ideas. Chances are you spend a good majority of your time fighting fires, leaving you with very little discretionary time for "nice to do" stuff like PM. As a peak-performance coach, I've seen this happen all too often.

Please hear me out when I say that what I'm about to offer next comes with the utmost respect and sincerity for your situation: Quit making excuses about not having time. You choose to make time for what you consider to be important. Making the time do to this is about making your superstars—one of your most valuable assets—a priority.

How did the business survive when you spent a week out of office for that family emergency? How is it you found time to untangle that key client issue when the account was in jeopardy? Have you had an instance when you stopped everything to keep that one superstar who threatened to quit if you didn't find a way to change a key process?

Alfred Adler, a prominent Austrian doctor, once said, "Life happens at the level of events, not of words. Trust movement." The key to your time management success is to say "no" to the right things.

Make an appointment with your superstar far in advance. Put it on your calendar and don't change it—ever! What if you had a company rule that the PM meetings were the only meetings that weren't allowed to be changed, shifted, or modified—except for genuine health emergencies and natural disasters? Even important customer meetings could come second to this small, sacred time slot. Remember, that is a choice you have.

Time Truth #2: 3 Percent of Your Time Shouldn't be Too Much to Ask

Below is a potential timeline for your PM meetings:

- 45 minutes for the initial mutual objective-setting conversation
- 30 minutes for the first 30-day check-in
- 60 minutes for the 60-day check-in
- 45 minutes for the formal 90-day evaluation
- 60 minutes (per quarter) for prep and documentation

The above totals four hours. Now let's say you have five superstars who report directly to you (requiring 20 hours of PM per quarter) and that, on average, you work ten hours a day. You'd need about two days out of every quarter, or 3 percent investment of your time, to keep your

MVAs finely tuned, focused, and optimally engaged. Given what you'd get in return, is spending four focused hours every 90 days on each superstar really too much to ask?

On a human level, your superstars need to feel important. Making the time to check in helps the team feel like they matter and also keeps your relationships fresh. I bet you currently spend more than four hours a week just casually browsing YouTube links, jokes, and silly chain letters.

The point here is that you *do* have the time. The question is, where are you choosing to spend it? If you're not spending a few productive hours per quarter focused on developing and supporting your superstars, you're risking a significant and expensive people problem.

If you're consistently finding that your PM conversations are taking longer than they should, split the time in half. Perhaps isolating the variables can point to the chatty culprit. Maybe they get the first block of time and you take the second block. In that way, you can share accountability for keeping the time focused.

Time Truth #3: It Costs You More Time Not to Do PM

In his groundbreaking book *The E-Myth,* Michael Gerber suggests that most SBOs are too busy working "in" the business instead of working "on" it. That means they are far too involved in baking cakes to effectively manage their delivery folks. Gerber realizes many SBOs are too busy to do critical strategic work because they're doing busy tactical work.

One common reason a SBO gets trapped in the details is because once upon a time she and a small team of doers were the whole business. As the business progressed, the SBO's strategic role didn't advance nearly as quickly as the business demanded. As a result, effective PM often takes a back seat, and roles and responsibilities between doers and overseers get fuzzy and redundant.

By not having a good PM program in place, you're *already* wasting more time than the program would require. How many times do you repeat yourself about the same issues? Have you lost sleep because you didn't trust a team member to do something, forcing you to take the task on yourself? That kind of bubble-up management approach costs you time, peace of mind, and ultimately your long-term freedom.

By not pushing the right stuff down, the wrong stuff bubbles up:

- What percent of your time gets hijacked by menial tasks?
- What don't you get to do because of those menial tasks?
- How frequently do you have to stay late, when everyone else goes home, just so you can do "the important" stuff?
- How would you know if you were spending too much time doing the wrong work?

Time Truth #4: You Can Swap Questions and Status Checks in Advance

Another easy way to make the time for check-ins is to send the status updates and feedback in advance. This way you can just focus on the relevant gaps during your discussions. Maybe you and your superstars work closely together and know each other very well. You may not need much more than a "hey, watch out for ______" kind of update.

By having your superstars bring written updates and feedback, they're pretty much giving you all the documentation you need for the formal evaluations. This minimizes the time you need to prepare for the evaluations, too. It doesn't get much faster than that, does it?

Time Truth #5: Not All Growth Is Good Growth

If, for whatever reason, you still can't find the time to do performance management with your team—congratulations! Business must be amazing for you. That means you should be able to afford a chief operating officer (COO). Hire one and let her do the PM with the team. You would then do the PM process with your COO. Be clear about how you would prefer your COO to keep you updated on the PM with your team. Stay close but not too close.

Remember that key question of knowing when you should hire more people? One possible answer to this question might be when you can no longer consistently and appropriately manage your direct reports. If the demands for your time consistently force you into reaction mode, think about other options. If you're not quite ready to hire a COO-level position, perhaps you could just promote someone from within to a team leader position.

However you do it, be sure to recognize when your business growth is outreaching your internal capacity. What indicators are you relying on to let you know when you should actually say "no" to more business opportunities? Your ability to do good, solid, performance management with your superstars could be one such indicator. You could create a people problem precisely because you're accepting too much business without installing the structure to support it.

As for actually rolling out the program, Figure 11.1 on page 178 shows a potential schedule, timeline, and some key discussion points that might be useful.

You can download this entire timeline from my website at www.christophermcintyre.com and modify it to fit your needs.

Figure 11.1—Chapter 11 Summary Checklist: The Rollout

ROLLING OUT YOUR PM PROGRAM		
Timing	**Activity**	**Notes / Actions**
180 days	Build your case	➡ See questions on page 170 to get you started
150 days	State your intent	➡ Have superstars read this book before next meeting ➡ Give team list of questions to think about ➡ Expect answered questions at next meeting
120 days	Enlist the team (overview meeting)	➡ Get team's thoughts about book ➡ Get team's ideas around your questions ➡ Loosely discuss your MVAs ➡ Loosely discuss systematic success formula ➡ Give team this timeline (modified to fit your needs) ➡ Have team fill in sections I & II of form for next meeting
90 days	Enlist the team (develop sections I & II of the PM form)	➡ Share thoughts on Sections I & II ➡ Agree on best ideas for Sections I & II ➡ Have team fill in Sections III thru IV of the form for next meeting
60 days	Enlist the team (develop sections III & IV of the PM form)	➡ Agree on best thoughts around Sections III thru IV ➡ Get agreement on format for 30-day check-ins ➡ Have superstars introduce the idea to employees ➡ Discuss how to roll out the program to employees ➡ Solicit employee ideas on the program ➡ Have superstars do self-assessment using new form for next meeting

Figure 11.1—**Chapter 11 Summary Checklist: The Rollout**, continued

Timing	Activity	Notes / Actions
30 days	Minor adjustments	➡ Discuss feedback from employees on program ➡ Tweak MVAs / success formula as necessary ➡ Agree on when to tweak program after rollout ➡ Clarify annual goals for superstars to develop during their first objective-setting conversation
The Big Day	Roll out program	➡ Have mutual objective-setting conversation ➡ Get great sleep tonight

Conclusion

Bringing It All Together

Business growth is good. Business growth, uncontrolled, is bad. Bad growth steals the creativity, excitement, emotional well-being, and ultimate freedom that business owners deserve.

Truly laying the foundation for freedom as you continue to grow your small business is a complex process. That process is made easier with the right team on board. Breaking down your people process means looking at how you get and keep talent. It also requires being as swift as possible when you absolutely must let someone go. With the right team you can let go of more tactical work and focus, strategically, where you should.

One often ignored key area—nearly invisible to the entire people process—is your distinct, systematic success message. That theme, or mantra, needs to be consistent and is core to protecting the brand of your business. Your mantra can be broken down into a formula that everyone understands and is directly connected to.

A performance management system provides that connection. This is where you clearly align business goals and superstar objectives with your most valuable assets. That will help keep consistent performance conversations focused on the most important issues. That focus, enables an empowered team guided by the anchor of a core success formula.

The Roadmap to Freedom starts with Book 1, installing a trusted infrastructure that *Connecting People to a Core Message*. Now it's time to oil the machine. The next book, Book 2: *Leading and Motivating without Money*, will give you a step-by-step process to do just that.

Thank you for taking the time to read this book. It's my sincere hope that it can, in some small way, help you to make what you do—easier! Now get to it. I salute you!

Part IV

Appendices

APPENDIX A

Meet the Heroes

Who: Dave Konstantin

Business Name: K-Co Construction

Type of Business: General contractor specializing in custom home and residential remodeling.

Based In: San Diego, California

Website: www.kcoconstruction.com

One cool quote from this interview: "I started the business in 1995 by myself with $800 to get it going. One of my goals was to not work with my nail bags and to be a manager as I had been with other companies. I achieved that within four months."

One thing I loved about this interview: Dave's entire interview was mind-blowing. When I was polling local colleagues for SBOs who might be good fits for my interviews, Dave's name was the only one to come up multiple times. Dave's story is the stuff movies are made of. He used to fly his own plane to smuggle drugs into the country, until that lifestyle led to his own addiction and ultimately to dumpster diving for food. Good thing for K-Co, and the community, Dave ultimately found Narcotics and Alcoholics Anonymous–and sobriety.

Since then, he's made such a difference in the lives of so many people that the city of San Diego actually named August 4, 2007, as "Dave Konstantin Day" for his "tireless civic and personal commitment to the community." Unfortunately, about a year after our interview, Dave was diagnosed with malignant mesothelioma and passed away on June 6th, 2012.

Because his story is so powerful, and to honor his achievements, I'm offering his interview for free download from my www.christophermcintyre.com. I encourage you to listen to it and then pass it on to a friend. It's unbelievably inspirational–and Dave is sincerely a true community hero and will be missed but his spirit will live on forever.

Who: Lynette Le Mere

Business Name: Pure Joy Catering

Type of Business: Full-service event catering

Based In: Santa Barbara, California

Website: www.purejoycatering.com

One key quote from this interview: "If you're going to do one thing–get it right."

One thing I loved about this interview: Two words: Focus, tenacity. Lynette represents that persevering, single-mother with an 8th-grade education success story that everyone loves to hear about. She (literally) started her award-winning business with just one pot in a borrowed kitchen. You can connect with Pure Joy Catering on Facebook.

Who: Shari Smith

Business Name: Green Field Paper Company

Type of Business: Tree-free handmade and machine-made hemp paper

Based In: San Diego, California

Website: www.greenfieldpaper.com

One cool quote from this interview: "We started by answering the phones."

One thing I loved about this interview: Shari's interview WOWED me. There's such a thing as tree-free paper? And "hemp" paper too? With her initial business model Shari somehow found a way to leverage her most critical employees, the paper makers, in part-time roles only.

Unlike any of the other SBOs I interviewed, Shari actually bought her business from someone else. The previous owner's process had been to consistently let phone calls go straight to voicemail and have employees return the calls at some designated point. Now that may sound odd to you—but someone, probably many people, decided that was an appropriate choice for the business. I highlighted Shari's quote about how she changed the business as a great reminder for you to stay curious about where you may be validating seemingly strange "choices" as well.

Who: Erwin Richter

Business Name: Polysport, Inc.

Type of Business: Sporting goods international exporter

Based In: Miami, Florida

One cool quote from this interview: "When I graduated with my MBA, the first thing I did was have a bonfire with all the finance books, and roasted marshmallows."

One thing I loved about this interview: Erwin and his wife, who are both immigrants to the United States, had no support systems in place. All they had was each other—and no choice but to succeed. His charisma and ability to develop, leverage, and maintain all sorts of relevant international relationships is amazing. And the way he forecasts future business needs, economic climates, and shifting international business costs is unbelievable.

Who: Dominic Carlos

Business Name: Four Seasons Lawn Aeration, Inc.

Type of Business: Lawn aerations

Based In: San Diego, California

Website: www.lawnaerating.com

One cool quote from this interview: "We had a customer that promised to stick with us until they died or got divorced. Divorce is the main thing that steals our business."

One thing I loved about this interview: Did you know what "aeration" meant? I didn't—and I know you wouldn't want me to ruin the surprise, so go look it up! What I loved about this interview was Dominic's simple, take-it-or-leave-it approach. No stress. His prospective customers either want the service or they don't. That laid-back attitude contributes to his easygoing high quality of life, which is something many SBOs would certainly like more of. Check out Dominic's hilarious "dog-test" for his new employee screening process.

Who: James Carter

Business Name: Be Legendary (formerly Repario)

Type of Business: Inspirational—focused on helping people rediscover themselves

Based In: Reno, Nevada

Website: www.belegendary.org

One cool quote from this interview: "One of the reasons I don't work out as much as I should is because I can't write things down, and I don't want to forget them."

One thing I loved about this interview: James was joking about the gym comment, to make a more serious point about not doing what we know we should do. James is literally in the business of creating and installing trust, confidence, and empowerment in individuals. That kind of job requires an individual whose "inner-work" is done–and James is definitely that guy. Be Legendary's "Building a Dream" programs to bring together businesses and disadvantaged youth are extraordinary. They've changed the lives of hundreds of thousands of people across the globe. Follow Be Legendary on Twitter and get connected on Facebook.

Who: Judy Lawton

Business Name: The Lawton Group (formerly TLC Staffing)

Type of Business: Full-service staffing, consulting, and employee solutions company

Based In: San Diego, California

Website: www.lawtongrp.com

One cool quote from this interview: "I started my illustrious career in the staffing industry, handing out punch, cookies, and coffee to old people who had nothing better to do than hang around at a savings and loan all day and watch their money grow."

One thing I loved about this interview: As if you couldn't tell from her quote, Judy's energy is contagious. She's open, nonjudgmental, and extremely caring for everyone around her. I was particularly attracted to how Judy was sensitive and responsive to the fact that corporate hiring managers often connected better with her younger team members. No ego—just an adjustment. She's a powerful, genuine leader, and the Lawton Group's consistent success proves it.

Who: Phil Coady

Business Name: Microgroove

Type of Business: Software development company focused on the entertainment industry

Based In: Seattle, Washington

Website: www.microgroove.com

One cool quote from this interview: "We have an internal motto: 'Yeah—it's a computer, it can do that.' Let's not hear about what it can't do, or what you tried and didn't work."

One thing I loved about this interview: I didn't want Phil's interview to end. He had an exceptional way of clearly articulating the conscious competence behind his leadership approach. He started his software development career with Microsoft, and when that job went away, he and his (now) wife decided they're rather do something cool together with friends. Welcome to Microgroove: founder of the world's single largest music-focused platform on the web.

Who: Jay Nelson

Type of Business: Heavy construction

Based In: New England

One cool quote from this interview: "People get fat, dumb, and happy. You take things for granted and the next thing you know—bang! It's all over with. You can't let yourself think that you've arrived."

One thing I loved about this interview: Jay was on his boat for the winter touring the southern U.S. coastal area. He's a hero in my mind for that alone. He's also a great example of a blue-collar guy, flexible enough to lead and motivate both blue- and white-collar workers. One minute, he's negotiating with chief executives for multimillion-dollar business deals. The next, he's inspiring his dump truck drivers to do their best work. This interview provided the ultimate contrast in the range of "right" leadership traits.

Who: Dr. Steven Jones

Business Name: Jones & Associates Consulting

Type of Business: Diversity and organizational change

Based In: San Diego, California

Website: www.jandaconsult.com

One cool quote from this interview: "We're trying to develop a system that counters the current system of oppression. Racism, sexism, and the other 'ism's' continue because they are amorphous and regenerative. We're talking about the air that we breathe. We're infusing healthy oxygen through positively appreciating each other."

One thing I loved about this interview: Steven's quote says it all. He's an illuminator, someone who makes the invisible visible. Having had the distinct privilege to work closely with him on a national scale, I've witnessed his genius personally. Steven works in the sticky, emotionally charged, and often invisible world of diversity consultation. Yet, he has a way of expressing ideas that makes even the most jaded and defensive people simply say, "Exactly!" That gift must be heard to be understood.

Who: David Stebbins

Business Name: The Stebbins Group

Type of Business: Lawyer and real estate tycoon

Based In: San Diego, California

Website: www.stebbinsgroup.com

One cool quote from this interview: "Being a college graduate, living with [your] grandmother, really makes you humble."

One thing I loved about this interview: David, a recovered addict, speaks about his success and his failures with a rare and refreshing level of raw honesty. I loved David's willingness to talk about what it's really like to be wealthy and about money in general. This interview has it all: temper, arrogance, humility, honesty, and relentless commitment to work harder than most people on the planet.

Appendix B

Key People Skills, Work Ethics, and Attributes (PEAs or Mantras)

PEOPLE SKILLS, WORK ETHICS, AND ATTRIBUTES (PEAs)		
Accountable	Effective	Capable at planning
Achiever	Efficient	Positive
Adaptable	Empathetic	Problem solver
Affectionate	Engaging	Productive
Available	Excellent	Protective
Calm	Expert	Quality
Committed	Flexible	Reconcile
Communicative	Healing	Reliable
Confident	Takes Initiative	Report
Cooperative	Inspiring	Resolved
Creative	Good leader	Resourceful
Decisive	Listener	Respectful
Dependable	Loyal	Willing to revise
Disciplined	Optimizing	Servant
Discoverer	Negotiator	Team worker
Driven	Passionate	Understanding
Educated	Persuasive	Utilizes assets

About the Author

Chris McIntyre is known internationally as a peak-performance expert. He graduated from Penn State with a BA in Business and Psychology and also holds dual MA's in HR Management and Development. He was a Captain in the Air Force, and led deployment operations for one of the Air Force's busiest F-16 Fighter Wings during 9/11.

Since separating from the military and starting his business in 2005, he's founded Southern California's first *Leadership Development Academy* specifically for the faith-based and nonprofit community.

He has addressed more than 100,000 people in 48 different states, and in India, Saudi Arabia, Dubai, and the UK. He's worked with senior executives across all industries ranging from *Fortune 100* organizations to leading small businesses and associations.

Chris's keynotes, public and private programs, and peak-performance consulting programs focus specifically on small-mid-sized businesses and organizations.

For more information, visit: www.christophermcintyre.com.

Index